ALONE AT HOME

by Marian Weston

P.O. Box 558, Exeter EX1 9FT

Copyright © 2007 Marian Weston

No part of this publication may be reproduced or transmitted in any form without the written permission from the publisher.

ISBN: 978-0-9555137-0-1

www.swifttransitions.co.uk

Written by Marian Weston

Edited by Zoe Meyer

Illustrations and book design by Graham Booth
www.chopperchoons.com

ACKNOWLEDGEMENTS

From the original idea to its ultimate publication 'Alone at Home' has been a long time in the making, and there are countless people to thank for helping bring it to fruition. There are some, however, without whose help in particular my dream would have remained just that, a dream.

Above all I would like to acknowledge the terrific contributions made by Robin Pascoe and Jo Parfitt. Robin provided me with the inspiration and encouragement to attempt this project in the first place. Her friendship, humour and mentoring through the entire process has been fantastic. Meanwhile, Jo has unstintingly committed her time, experience and patience, and provided words of encouragement when the going got tough. I was extremely fortunate to have enjoyed such support, particularly in view of their acknowledged expertise in their respective fields.

I am most grateful to Dr Greg Guldner for contributing such a thoughtful and touching Foreword. And to Lois Bushong and Connie Moser for their insightful contributions to the book.

I am indebted to all those whom I have spoken to within the 'short- term assignment' world, who have tirelessly answered my many questions and shared their research and experiences. In particular I wish to thank the numerous 'stay-at-home' spouses, who through their enthusiastic response to my questionnaires and willingness to share their experiences, have helped to give our community a voice. I would like to believe that their contributions will ensure that the role of the family within the short-term assignment scenario has, at last, been given the profile I passionately believe it deserves.

Publication of 'Alone at Home' would not have been possible without the editing expertise I received from Zoe Meyer, and Graham Booth's creativity with the illustrations and typesetting.

Indeed I would like to thank all those from within my network - your support has been invaluable. Most importantly, however the biggest debt is owed to my own family, Andrew, James and Laura, who have often served as my raw material. Certainly our experiences together have provided the core inspiration for this book. Thank you for your love and motivation.

FOREWORD

Over the last thirty years, the industrialized world has experienced a gradual but steady increase in the number of couples and families who choose, or otherwise find themselves in, a geographically separated relationship. Historically a dilemma seen primarily in military families, separations now occur within a vast array of civilian occupations. Virtually all multi-national companies and governmental agencies require some degree of geographical relocation for certain segments of their workforce. Some of these separations are short term, lasting a few weeks to months, while others may last several years. In the not so long ago past, couples and families typically moved en masse when one member was summoned overseas. Now, more couples and families choose instead to try a long-distance relationship.

Once thought of as an oddity, geographically separated relationships have slowly achieved the status of a viable, albeit misunderstood, alternative. While surveys still show that most people believe geographical separation places a relationship at risk, society has come to at least tolerate those who choose this path. The frequency of articles in magazines and newspapers, coupled with the growing number of books on the topic reveal an increasing desire to better understand and cope with these relationships.

Not surprisingly, research on the topic of geographical separation also has increased and has revealed some surprising results. For example, despite common opinion, the majority of studies have shown that long-distance relationships appear to have the same rates of success as geographically close relationships. Thus, they can indeed work.

Nevertheless, couples in separated relationships face relatively unique issues compared to geographically close couples. Historically these couples would learn to cope with these issues through trial and error. Fortunately resources for these couples are now appearing on the internet and in printed publications. These sources hope to guide couples in these relationships around traditional struggles faced when separated.

Marian Weston's book continues in this tradition by providing a resource for geographically separated couples and families. She writes in a tone that is not overly academic or pretentious, but rather as someone who has been through separation, experienced the challenges, learned from struggles, and now shares her wisdom with the reader. The journey feels much like a chat with a good friend. This parallels research on geographical separation that suggests an experienced confidante helps mitigate the stress of being apart. While the book obviously cannot take the place of such a person, it certainly seems to help calm the nerves and soothe the soul of those who find themselves apart from loved ones.

Marian's book provides a relatively unique resource, in that it addresses both couples and families, focusing at times on dealing with children and their specific needs during separation. While this issue has been well discussed among military families, the same is not true for civilian separations and this represents a welcome addition.

Couples in geographical separations require both "tactical" and "strategic" support. Tactical support refers to the more practical day-to-day issues such as learning when and how to make contact with your partner, determining which cellular phone contract will best suit your needs, discussing how to deal with chores that have traditionally been the responsibility of the person leaving, and so forth. Strategic support provides more long term stability by helping couples to see the big picture and determine where they should focus their efforts. For example, research shows that separated couples must communicate with one another about the apparently trivial, day-to-day issues in their lives, rather than focus exclusively on the emotional components such as telling one another how much they miss and love them. Similarly, couples must stay optimistic that geographically separated relationships represent an acceptable and indeed robust choice, despite a preponderance of negativity from many in the society.

These two targets – communication about day-to-day events and staying optimistic – exemplify strategic support for separated couples. Marian's book aptly combines both elements of support providing broad strategic goals and down-to-earth practical advice to help sustain separated relationships.

Couples who find themselves faced with the specter of separation would do well to seek and embrace the wisdom of those who have traveled the same path. Such wisdom resides in the pages that follow.

Gregory Guldner, MD, MS
Director
Center for the Study of Long Distance Relationships in Southern California
Author, Long Distance Relationships

Contents

Introduction **15**

Chapter 1 - The Support Network **19**

    We all need support
    My story
    Repatriation trauma
    The Power of positive thinking
    How colourful is your garden?
    The lifestyle is cyclical
    Fire fighting
    Different types of support

Part One – Practical Support **25**

    Lighten your load
    Domestic dilemmas
    Your network becomes a team
    Useful information

Part Two –Emotional Support **31**

    Introduction
    The importance of friends
    Close family
    The sandwich generation
    Quality time for yourself
    Health and exercise
    Introducing coaching into your life
    Career coaching
    A Pause for reflection
    Role models
    Goal setting
    A helping hand
    Discover your confidence
    Re-invent yourself
    Are you ready for a change?
    Each support network is individual and important

Part Three – Researching and creating your network **41**

    Introduction
    Get creative
    Questions to ask
    Don't be shy
    Advice from the expert
    Support network exercises

Part Four - Coping Strategies and Helpful hints 45

    What social life?
    Group activities
    Be flexible and have lots of coping strategies
    The empty nest
    A gentle warning
    The sky is the limit
    Think big
    A positive process
    Supporting at a distance
    Feedback
    Family feedback
    Quick tips

Chapter 2 - Relationships and Communications 53

    Introduction
    Communicate regularly it helps keep the balance
    Skype and email contact
    Let the technology work for you
    Learning to share
    How long are you home for?
    What do you tell them?
    What do you miss?
    Re-entry and the cutlery drawer scenario
    Giving time out
    Constant re-adjustment
    Are you prepared?
    Questions to be considered pre-assignment
    Discuss together the negatives and compromises which will have to be made pre-assignment
    Organisation and pre-planning for assignees return leave is essential
    Organise regular trips home it helps the planning process
    The assignee can feel disconnected from home
    Social lives when your partner is back
    Encourage teenage children to visit in posting
    Worrying and the what ifs?'
    Children and discipline
    The Shh word - Sex
    Marriage counselling
    Infidelity
    Marriage breakdown
    Substance abuse
    Debt and gambling
    Visit your partner in posting it gives you valuable couple time
    Ill health
    Redundancy
    What's on offer
    Family feedback
    Quick tips
    Relationships and communications checklist

Chapter Three - Education and Schools 71

Introduction
Researching schools
Take the time to establish good lines of communication with the school
Keep the school informed of personal circumstances
Deal with difficulties quickly
Complaints proceedure
Become conversant with homework/coursework schedule
Diarise school meetings
Pre-plan partner's return trips to coincide with school functions
Emergency contact
Pre-exam anxieties?
International Schools
Private independent schools within the UK
The house system
The state system within the UK
Family feedback
Quick tips

Chapter 4 - Family Responsibilities 81

Introduction
Be flexible and intuitive
Review your priorities regularly
The sandwich generation
Regularly re-acquaint yourself with your children
Kids and their social lives
Encourage independence
Ground rules
Resentment
Get rid of the guilt
Quality family time
Find a friend
Create extra time and space
Get cooking
Be prepared
Feedback from the kids
Quick tips

Chapter 5 - Finances and Budgeting 89

    Pre-planning
    Doing homework
    Get organised
    Accounting systems
    The best way to pay
    Authorisation
    The serious stuff – Wills and Legal issues
    Insurance
    Uncertainty
    Financial goals
    Reading the small print – your responsibilities
    Financial update
    Family feedback

The Epilogue 97

About the Author 101

Recommendations 102

INTRODUCTION

I know the next few months are going to be the most testing period to date of my career as a 'stay-at-home' partner. My husband, Andrew has just left to start a new project overseas and will be away for three months. Our two teenagers, James aged eighteen years and Laura aged sixteen years, are about to sit 'A' level and 'GCSE' exams (major public exams).

My emotions are mixed: poignant trepidation, pierced by the sharp realisation that the scenario which is short term assignments is emotional, erratic, frustrating, interesting and often lonely.

To successfully live this lifestyle to the maximum, you have to be a bit of a chameleon, independent and tenacious, a survivor, constantly changing and blending with your environment.

When our family first encountered the short term assignment experience over five years ago, we were naïve and totally unprepared! Assuming the challenges would be similar to those we had experienced as expatriates was our first mistake. Many mistakes and five years later, our naivety and enthusiasm has proved both presumptuous and productive.

My intention in writing this book has been to create something tangible, a practical tool for those experiencing this particular lifestyle. Although this has been written from the British perspective, I hope it will resonate with a global audience. Wherever you are based in the world, the challenges we experience as the 'stay-at-home' partner will be similar. I am writing this hoping that within these pages you will find practical support, friendship and encouragement, something to reach for when the going gets tough.

Welcome to the world of short term assignment working!

CHAPTER ONE
The Support Network

We all need support:

We all need that reassurance there is someone to lean on, don't we? Someone to call on in a hurry when the kids need a lift from school or a good neighbour to pop in and feed the cat when you are away on holiday. Someone to turn to for help in a crisis. On gloomy, rainy days we feel an even greater need for someone else to chat to, or occasionally rely on. The simple knowledge that a trusted friend is next door, perhaps just around the corner, can help so much towards feeling settled and belonging.

I recently found the following definitions of the words 'support' and 'network' in the Oxford Dictionary. 'Support' was defined as: 'to hold in position so as to keep from falling, sinking or slipping.' Whilst the definition for 'network' was: 'something resembling an openwork fabric or structure – an extended group of people with similar interests or concerns who interact and remain in informal contact for mutual assistance or support'. These definitions combined provide a good description of the 'stay-at-home' partner.

The support network is especially important for the 'stay-at-home' partner. In the not-so-distant past it was natural for the family unit to live close by and as a matter of course provide a practical and emotional support network. The 'stay-at-home' partner remaining in the home country felt no need to look any further a field than the safety net of their own extended family. However, the pace of change in our lives today, led by technology and globalisation means that our support network needs are also changing fast and exceed what the extended family could offer. So they should be regularly reviewed to ensure the 'stay-at-home' is listened to and cared for appropriately.

My story:

If, like me for instance your partner's decision to start short-term work coincides with repatriation, the support network at home can be limited. Repatriation is always a culture shock for the whole family, but coping with repatriation and Andrew starting short-term assignment working was a double whammy! Although moving back into our own house in a familiar area helped, the practical chores of furnishing the house, choosing schools, settling the children was not unlike going to a new posting. Several weeks into our repatriation, the euphoria of being at home was beginning to wear off. Boxes had been unpacked, six weeks of school holidays still remained to be filled, siblings were arguing, and I was grappling with alternating feelings of terror and inadequacy, striving to grasp the mechanics of life in the UK after an absence of ten years.

Repatriation trauma:

Feeling at a distinctly low ebb and in dire need of talking to another adult, I found some old issues of the magazine 'Woman Abroad' in my packing boxes. Gail Macindoe's feature on coaching stirred my curiosity. A former expatriate and business coach, Gail's article highlighted the benefits of coaching and the offer of a complimentary coaching session was tempting. Frantic to re-connect with another expatriate, I phoned. Her friendly, direct manner and understanding of my particular situation, thanks to her twenty plus years expatriate experience ensured that we were soon talking like old friends, discovering mutual acquaintances and interests. On reflection this contact with Gail was my introduction to coaching and the foundation of my support network. The coaxing and cajoling I received from Gail during our coaching sessions was productive, humorous and greatly helped boost my confidence.

A very welcome phone call from an old school friend, now living in our local area also helped me in those early days. Sue and I had been at boarding school together so shared not only the Third Culture Kid (TCK) experience, but having also lived abroad for most of her adult life she knew the difficulties I was encountering. That contact proved a huge support early in our repatriation. Just knowing there was no pressure on you to give vast explanations, or act like everything was fine, you were talking to someone who understood. As well as providing me with a vent for my emotions, it was also great for our kids. Talking to Sue's teenage son, they discovered the emotions and difficulties they were encountering were normal, they weren't unique or different.

The power of positive thinking:

Although I had moved back to a known area, friends we had known before going abroad were limited. Some had moved away, others were too busy getting on with their lives to be concerned with our return. In those early days of repatriation it was tough and lonely. Life in England had changed dramatically during our ten year absence abroad. I felt alien and overwhelmed. Desperately needing to feel I belonged somewhere, I realised the answer was to re-connect with people who had similar experiences to mine. Several months after my phone call to Gail, I attended two workshops in London run by dual-career expert and writer, Jo Parfitt. I was seriously connecting with a variety of people, some having expatriate and short-term assignment experiences similar to my own, others addressing career and lifestyle challenges. And interestingly, all those I connected with shared one aspect in common - they were not only expatriates but also entrepreneurial. Meeting these entrepreneurial expatriates was not only enlightening but also a reminder that I had similar skills and experience. All I needed was confidence and to focus on a range of prospects and explore them. This realisation turned out to be the start of my new writing career which has constantly challenged, excited and frustrated me. My decision to research and develop the subject of single-status assignments as it affects the 'stay-at-home' partner led me to write articles for expatriate publications. I attended and wrote reports on several conferences as well as giving pre-assignment briefings and workshops for expatriates. Writing this book seemed a natural progression.

Several months ago I was ecstatic and felt a contented glow of personal satisfaction. My proposal to participate in the 2007 Families in Global Transition Conference (www.figt.org) had been accepted by the Conference Board. Most significantly it has meant that as I have gained confidence, I have become more adventurous with the added advantage of an ever increasing support network.

How colourful is your garden?

Support networks are in fact a vital and integral part of our lives. Just as we nurture our plants with fertiliser, plant food, water, pruning, slug pellets and pride without which we would not have a healthy, colourful and productive garden, so indeed support networks sustain and nurture us in much the same way. It is especially important not to lose sight of this aspect of your daily life at a time when you are coping on your own. Just because you have all the responsibility for running home and family most of the time, you will be fooling no-one but yourself if you think you can do it all alone. Like our gardens, by sharing the load and working on building strong support systems you will enhance your family life, improve your health and enjoy your leisure time by sharing the load more fully.

If you are the sporadic-gardener type, not used to planning ahead and only watering and feeding the flowers when they are already drooping, your family situation and personal well-being will resemble a wilting garden producing timid colour rather than the vivid, healthy and inviting space that you had been aiming for.

I can speak from my own personal experience that this is the very probable outcome of lack of attention to your own personal well-being and a fire-fighting attitude towards the inevitable domestic problems you have to face. So busy was I with my coping strategies that I was a prime example of the sporadic gardener, lurching from one drama to another, watering and feeding in a desperate attempt to revive my flagging garden (family). All my life I have been practical and organised, a coper was how I saw myself. But appearances can be deceptive. Whilst outwardly I was capable and coping, apparently efficiently, weathering the highs and lows (of which there were many) swanlike, gliding effortlessly and serenely through the water, the reality was quite different. The complex and difficult situation I was constantly faced with was taking its toll and beneath the surface I was in fact paddling desperately just to keep afloat.

Life with teenagers can be challenging at the best of times. Throw into that equation the support void created by the prolonged absences of your partner on short-term assignments, then it is hardly surprising that the resulting mayhem has a devastating impact, both at a practical and an emotional level.

The lifestyle is cyclical:

One of the first things you learn as you struggle to keep your head above water is that this lifestyle is cyclical; the cycle starts with advance preparations and then your partner departing on assignment. The family now can get a home routine organised. The first few weeks pass without too much incident and by now everyone is used to the new routine. In fact you may be giving yourself a pat on the back for coping well. The reality, however, was that we were living life constantly on the edge. It only took a minor issue to quickly upset the delicate balance and for a while family life became miserable, with everyone feeling angry and resentful. Part of our family was missing, with no third party to defuse the situation or see the other's point of view. We all seemed to do a lot of shouting! The atmosphere would for a while become strained, everyone would get the angst out of their system and things would calm down, until the next time!

Fire-fighting:

Whilst I had indeed got used to dealing with everything that came my way during my husband, Andrew's prolonged working absences over the last five years, my coping strategy was that of a fire fighter, reacting to each situation, putting out the flames before moving on to the next emergency. It had certainly taken its toll on me personally. I felt like an island, alone and totally responsible, the only one who could deal with things. I didn't need anyone else. Coping had become my 'raison d'etre' (fixation) and it was unhealthy. I realised that only by giving myself permission to slow down and let go could I change the situation.

Different types of support:

The support network of the 'stay-at-home' naturally divides into the following categories:

1) Practical help: gardener, cleaner, handyman, babysitter, car maintenance, computer maintenance and other parents sharing the school run duties. It encompasses every individual who helps you with the smooth running of your home.

2) Emotional support: This is provided by family, friends and counsellors and is both extremely necessary and important for the 'stay-at-home' partner. Whether your partner is away on assignment for a week or several months at a time, knowing that you have good emotional support is a huge comfort and will really benefit your family. Recognising the need for and actually giving individual family members opportunities to offload to others outside the close family unit, creates much-needed space as well as encouraging good communication.

3) Group support: Affiliated with personal interest, clubs or church provide a niche place where you meet up on a regular basis and experience a comforting sense of belonging. This not only helps your self-esteem and self-confidence, thereby contributing to an inner sense of well-being but also provides an extra safety net.

PART ONE
Practical Support

Lighten your load:

You have to be practical and realistic. Things you once viewed as luxuries may now be a necessity. If finances permit, I strongly recommend that you consider employing either a gardener or cleaner.

Make a list of chores your partner did pre-departure. Identify those chores which realistically you can tackle yourself and outsource the others. It is simply not possible to do everything and whilst lessening your load, in the long-term it keeps you sane and the family balanced. Your strengths will be needed 100% to concentrate on supporting the family. It is very easy to be undermined by the endless list of jobs to do, especially if you always have to consider budgets and finances.

Domestic dilemmas:

I enjoyed the day-to-day running of the house, but the mention of home maintenance or decorating was enough to bring me out in a cold sweat and make Andrew very nervous. Any creative instincts I nurtured were quickly nipped in the bud with Andrew's insistence that I quickly find a good decorator. I built up a network of recommended tradesmen through a combination of friends, local contacts and papers. Domestic emergencies such as the boiler or faulty plumbing flooding the house, inevitably happens when your partner has just left for his next assignment! So be prepared and have a list of recommended trade's people to hand for when an emergency arises. The computer until very recently had always been an enigma to me and was treated with due reverence. All electrical equipment has the uncanny knack of breaking down at the most inconvenient times and my computer was no exception. Frustrated by the amount of money I was spending on computer repairs and dependence on 'the expert' to fix even the most minor repairs, I did some homework and read several basic computer manuals. This was really helpful as it not only gave me some background information on computers, it also made me aware of potential problems, giving me the confidence to attempt to sort the problem before phoning the computer repair man. It was extremely satisfying when I was able to sort out a few basic computer problems unaided.

Your network becomes a team:

It is wise to try and use people you are comfortable with, in the house and are also recommended. When I was researching this network, I found it helpful to list a few important criteria which would help me make my choice:

- Efficiency at providing quotation
- Hourly rate
- Did I feel comfortable in the person's presence?
- Was he/she trustworthy?
- Would I feel happy for him/her to work alone in my house?
- Was his/her appearance neat, clean and businesslike?
- Was his/her vehicle and materials neat, clean and businesslike?
- Did he/she provide references?
- Was he/she a member of a reputed Guild?

As often happens, we got to know Graham, our decorator accidentally. He was helping the interior designer fit window blinds in our new house. His work was neat and efficient and he was discreet and very reliable. As I knew Graham lived locally I asked if he knew of a decorator he could recommend. He mentioned that his services also included house renovation and decoration so we didn't look any further.

Jason, who provides our garden maintenance service is cheerful, reliable, equally efficient with both routine garden tasks and major landscaping.

Over the past few years I have built up a strong rapport with both Graham and Jason. I find it very reassuring knowing that in the event of an emergency, I have such reliable people in the background.

USEFUL INFORMATION

Frustrated at never being able to find important information and contact numbers, I got organised and compiled a list of all our necessary useful contacts. I am sure that I am not the only one who struggles with organisation and therefore thought it would be a useful addition.

Short-Term Assignee Details

Partner/spouse contact details:

Postal Address: ....

E mail Address: ....

Telephone Number: .... Mobile Number: ....

Passport Details: ....

Medical Insurance Details: ....

Company Details/Contact Name: ....

Leave Dates: ....

Family Celebrations: ....

School Functions: ....

Assignee Insurance Details: ....

Professional Organisations: ....

Health:

Emergency Doctor's Number: ....

Emergency Hospital's Number: ....

Family Doctor: ....

Hospital: ....

Dentist: ....

Optician: ....

Specialist: ....

Medical Insurance Details: ....

Legal:

Bank Details: ....

Building Society Details: ....

Standing Orders/Direct Debits: ....

Credit Card Addresses: ....

Solicitor: ....

Location of Wills: ....

Financial Advisor: ....

Mortgage Details: ....

House:

Emergency Contact Details: ....

House Insurance Details: ....

Personal Insurance Details: ....

Water Provider: ....

Power Provider: ....

Telephone Provider: ....

Mobile Company: ....

Internet Provider: ....

Local Council: ....

Boiler Servicing Details: ....

Electrician: ....

Library: ....

Plumber: ....

Computer Technician: ....

Gardening Services: ....

Decorator: ....

Club: ....

Hairdresser: ....

Natural Therapist: ....

Church: ....

Relatives: ....

Friends: ....

Car:

Car Insurance Details: ....

Car Breakdown Insurance Details: ....

Vehicle Servicing Details: ....

Servicing Garage: ....

Children:

School: ....

Clubs: ....

Friends: ....

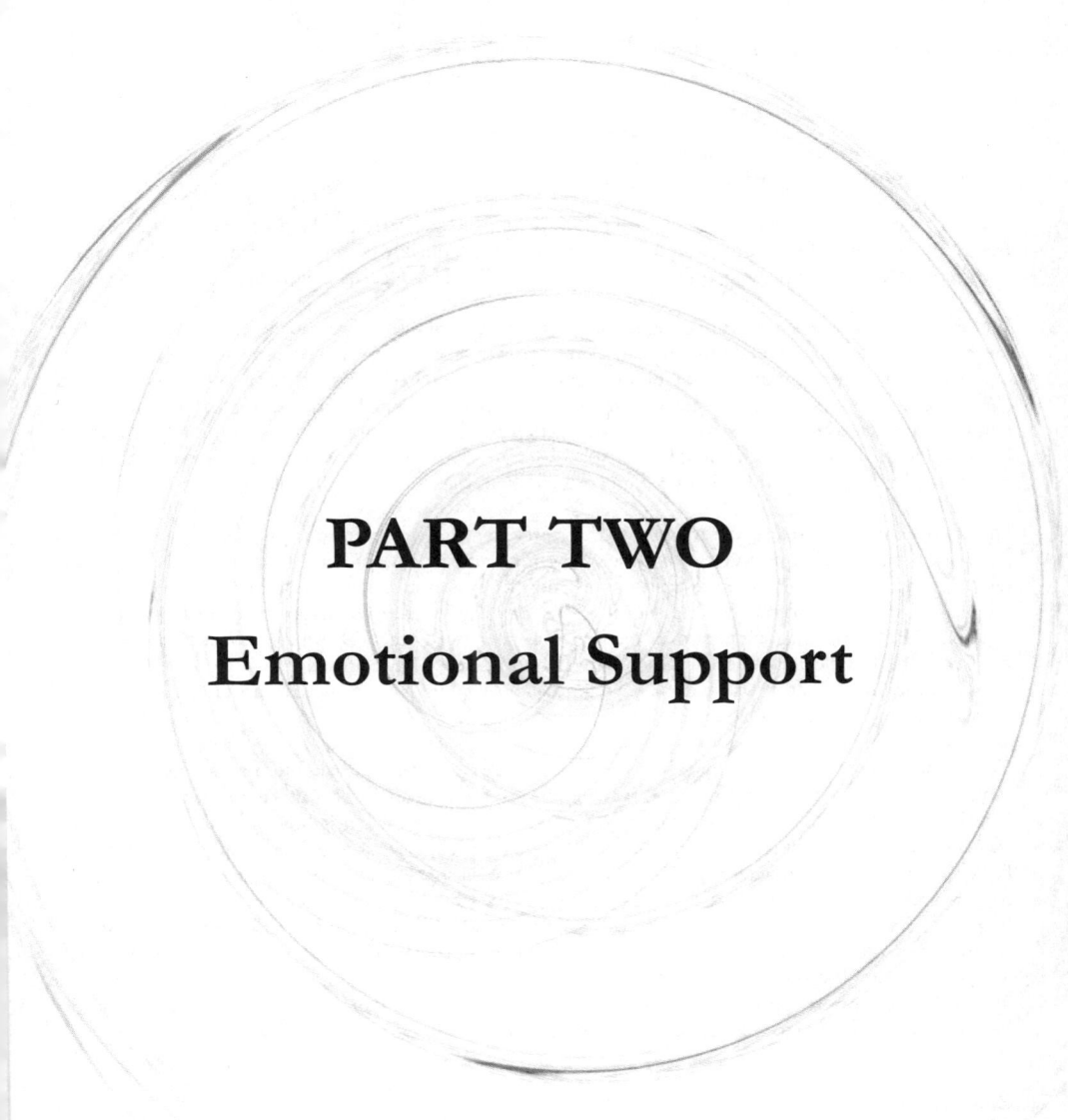

PART TWO
Emotional Support

Introduction:

It is really important when you are coping alone that you have a good emotional support network. Because most of your time is spent supporting the family and assignee, there is not a lot of spare time to concentrate on your personal well-being. The range your emotional support network can cover is very diverse and may include family, friends, doctors, complementary therapists, counsellors, school teachers and possibly even work colleagues. I talk more about the support of doctors/counsellors later in Part Two.

The importance of friends:

A bedrock of support to our family during our years of short term working has been Tina, a family friend. We first met when the children were very young and quickly bonded. Our circumstances closely matched; children of similar ages, living in the same road and both of us having been expatriates.

When we went overseas with our young family fourteen years ago there was no email, but Tina and I kept up the contact, writing several times a year. Although we were not regular correspondents, Tina's letters, overflowing with her quirky sense of humour and sporadic updates of family news were fun to read and great morale boosters. There was never a dry eye when we read Tina's letters, we laughed too much. Our annual summer leaves were often rounded off with a few days visiting Tina and her family at home in Devon. Picnics to local beaches and beauty spots were regular features of our stay and eagerly anticipated by James and Laura who found it a welcome change from the heat of the Middle East.

Having been married to a serviceman for many years, Tina was well used to coping alone with home and family responsibilities. She could empathise with our circumstances. When Andrew started doing short-term assignments abroad, often away for three months at a time, Tina's friendship and experience was an invaluable support to me, especially during the early days of our repatriation when everything was a struggle. Her unwavering support over the years has been both practical and emotional. Knowing there was someone I could talk to, have a moan and who understood the lifestyle was a boon. With a busy family home life herself, it was a great relief knowing that Tina was in the background, quiet, practical and nothing ever too much trouble.

Earlier this year whilst deliberating whom to appoint as guardian for our daughter Laura now at boarding, school I was stuck. My family lived too far away and so after much reflection, Tina was my only option. I hesitated perhaps a little, aware it was not a responsibility to be taken lightly and she already had her own family responsibilities. But I should have saved myself the worry. Her home has always been like a second home to our teenagers and now with two of her own at boarding school, she knew the routine and was a willing volunteer. Not one to fluster easily, she was the ideal choice, instantly lifting a huge load from my shoulders. Over the years her support has been practical and unwavering. She has several times willingly hosted the children for short periods, freeing me up to visit Andrew in posting as well as providing last minute cover when I have needed to go on unplanned business trips. This is the most valuable support you need when your partner is away, someone practical, reliable and level-headed because you often have to call for help at the last minute.

Close family:

Despite our family living at a distance we have been fortunate and have enjoyed strong support from them. Mum would sometimes come and stay if I was away for a few days, providing an adult presence in the house for our teenagers.

Duncan, my younger brother and his family have also been an integral part of our support network although living permanently in Switzerland. Having two teenagers themselves, they like me were experiencing the realities of life with teenagers and could empathise. Regular chats on the phone and email contact were great for offloading and invitations to visit during school holidays was a huge boon, welcomed by all of us. Everyone benefited from these visits. The kids were able to see and regularly re-connect with their cousins which has not only widened their sense of family, but has also given them a wonderful opportunity to establish strong relationships with them which will, I know, prove steadfast throughout their adult lives. Sometimes they visited on their own, giving me a bit of breathing space from the regular routine and responsibilities. If we visited en-famille, it gave us all a new lease of life. We were really privileged, their charming home in the Swiss mountains offering our kids more freedom than Devon suburbia. Able to cycle and swim in the summer and ski and toboggan in the winter, they were always outside and active. Benefiting by being away from our normal environment and from interactions with others, these breaks gave us all some very necessary and welcome breathing space. The kids had the companionship of their cousins and I had other adults to talk to.

Last summer, both my teenagers were away visiting their cousins in Switzerland for the week and this gave me the luxury of small chunks of uninterrupted time. Able to slow down, I sat in the garden, read a book, caught up on some writing. Utilising those few days to re-charge was brilliant, a welcome break in routine and environment, for me and our teenagers. Being free from the oft tight confines our family had become since Andrew had been working away was hugely beneficial. Everyone enjoyed their respective quality time and when we re-grouped we were all much more relaxed and had a great time catching up on each others news.

Don't be a martyr if you are presented with the opportunity of the children or you having some time away, either to friends or grandparents, school trips. Just take it, everyone will benefit.

The sandwich generation:

Your responsibilities may also include supporting elderly parents. This will inevitably put added strain on your emotional and physical resources as I discovered recently when my mother had to go into hospital for a major knee operation. Having always been fiercely independent and active, her operation was a learning curve for us all. A slow recovery and severe pain combined with Mum's frustration at her loss of activity and dependence on others did not make for happy bed fellows. With no immediate family nearby, working part-time, supporting Mum in hospital as well as maintaining our home/family balance, my juggling skills were hard pressed. It was a difficult period and simply not sustainable for long. Although I didn't have the presence and support of my brothers to help with the daily responsibilities of coping with Mum's hospitalisation and recuperation, both living long distances away, I did have regular telephone and email contact which helped. I could update them and this helped me offload.

Intuitively knowing I would be struggling with all the different responsibilities my younger brother Duncan came over for a week with his family. They hired a holiday cottage locally and took over some of the hospital visiting responsibilities. It was so nice to share, being able to hand over to someone else and not be totally responsible.

It made me realise that, for the most part because I am so used to coping alone my life was like a spinning top always in perpetual motion, not knowing how to stop.
Being given permission and the opportunity to slow down was a good lesson and made me do some serious evaluating. I needed to create more 'me time' and I immediately started prioritising on the home front. The first step was to say 'No' more often, allocating domestic chores more equally, generally loosening the reins. These simple steps really helped me. The kids became more responsible, it lessened my feelings of guilt and pressure and focused me superbly on my writing.

Quality time for yourself:

It is vital that in order to continue supporting the family you build regular quality time for yourself into your schedule. There is no need to worry that it will be to the detriment of the children.

Whether it is lunch with a friend, a walk along the beach, visiting an art gallery, the list is personal and endless. Your personal 'time out' is something to be viewed holistically. The simple things can give a lot of pleasure and so 'time for you' does not have to equate with extravagance or cost.

Health and exercise:

It is easy to make excuses not to exercise or put it off but you need that release with a physical workout to keep yourself fit and healthy. It then follows that it will be much easier to keep a good life-balance and stay well. Gym, tennis, swimming or yoga are all easily available locally.

Another arm to your network can be your doctor. An understanding doctor is a great boon, someone with whom you and your family have a good rapport. Pre-assignment I always found it a useful exercise to update our doctor, advising him of the work situation. I have found that establishing a good relationship with your doctor is especially important if you have teenagers. Teens don't want parents to interfere, but if you know they have someone with empathy and with whom they can confide in, this too helps lessen your total responsibility.

Maintenance both of physical and mental health is one of the most crucial factors for the 'stay-at-home' partner. Often it is the case that you are so tuned in to the rest of the family's issues that your own get forgotten. As soon as you realise you are starting to struggle, it is much better to make an appointment for a general discussion. Often the very fact that you have talked your worries over with another adult will have an immediate calming effect.

Remember you are doing a very difficult job. Don't kid yourself that you have to go it totally alone if you are feeling submerged, make an appointment and get outside help, from school, family doctor or counsellor. If you are sensible and recognise that from time to time this will be a normal need, it will not only maintain your health but that of your families too. Depression and fatigue are common issues for the 'stay-at-home' partner and only too frequently this occurs because it is not dealt with effectively at the start. You have to take control of your life, by being focused. Creating a healthy lifestyle for your family is of paramount importance.

A good way to start is to build a healthy diet and exercise regime into the family's schedule. It is easy to let things overwhelm you, cue fatigue and depression. I viewed maintaining home and family balance as my personal Everest, using my support network as metaphorical handholds in my ascent. Although I was often tempted to rush ahead to get to the top of my mountain, common sense did finally prevail. Going at a slower pace and supported my ascent was more fun, achieving and sustainable.

Introducing coaching into your life:

I was well aware of the benefits of coaching, having had both personal and business coaching sessions myself in the past. Listening to a talk by personal and business coach Ann Ross of New Perspectives Coaching (www.newperspectivescoaching.co.uk) at a local business women's network. I was intrigued; Anne's approach was slightly different. A successful and established personal coach, Ann is a qualified EFT (Emotional Freedom Therapy) therapist, cleverly combining both skills to provide both intuitive and focused support.

Ann explained to us: 'EFT is like psychological acupuncture without the needles.' Meeting Ann occurred during a period when I was struggling in my role as the 'stay-at home' partner. My life was constantly programmed to fast forward; there was little time to stop. Curiosity overcame my cautious nature and I booked an introductory session. My first impression was the peaceful atmosphere. Ann's room was simply furnished and her gentle, intuitive manner further enhanced the tranquillity. Describing the technique in more detail Ann explained: 'It can eliminate many emotional imbalances such as fears, phobias, trauma and panic attacks or anxiety. It works well for limiting beliefs, exam nerves and peak performance. It is a great relaxation technique that relieves stress in minutes.' According to Ann; 'The global medical profession has begun to open its mind to the technique. Doctors, psychologists and many therapists worldwide are now building it into their practices because of the positive outcomes' she said. Bolstered by the knowledge that it was a natural technique reassured me. It was at least worth a try. My scepticism was short lived. The sessions were immensely helpful and gave me the opportunity to de-stress and offload to Ann, who was an interested and intuitive observer. As well as providing me with the skills to recognise when I was feeling pressurised, she taught me some simple, natural techniques enabling me to instantly reduce the pressure on myself and my family. This awareness and the learnt skills have now become a new kind of support network.

The knowledge that I have regular sessions with Anne to look forward to, as well as the background support of emails/telephone calls to Ann have both helped me enormously. The importance of this ongoing support was demonstrated to me when I had two teenagers at home about to take major exams. The hormonally-charged atmosphere, full of different emotions and high anxiety levels was reaching an unbearable pitch. The techniques I had been taught were useful and calming, helping me to recognise and avoid many unnecessary confrontations. I knew if I needed an extra boost I could always phone Ann, either to book a session or have a chat. This was incredibly supportive during the six weeks of exams and precisely because I myself was more relaxed, so were the children, helping us to melt away many of our anxieties.

Career Coaching:

Having met and listened to several career coaches present during the 6th Annual W.I.N. (Women's International Networking) Conference in October 2003, I knew that if I was going to make this book a reality, it would be necessary to get some structured help, so I chose a career coach.

When choosing a career coach, intuition was my guide. Researching the W.I.N. website, I found several coaching services recommended by W.I.N. participants and phoned Veronique Beltz, of PeopleEdge Coaching (www.peopleedge.ch). The combination of her friendly disposition, sense of humour and focused coaching style convinced me she was the best person to advise and help me.

I organised weekly sessions a combination of telephone coaching interspersed with email contact over a period of three months. These sessions, were highlights in my diary and benefited me on two fronts: helping develop my confidence and skill in attempting this book and something special I was doing for myself, to look forward to. These regular sessions provided support, encouragement and motivation and because it was a regular date factored into my diary, gave me a positive focus, helping me better manage my time by giving my weeks some structure. Having the opportunity for a change in my normal routine and talking to another adult about issues totally unrelated to the normal home and family responsibilities was stimulating and refreshing.

Veronique is now an integral part of my support network and we email regularly. When I hit a low point with the book, I was trying to source more families with experience of short term work. The response did not meet my expectations and feeling de-motivated and disappointed, I emailed Veronique and had a moan. This is where generosity of spirit and goodwill steps forward. Whilst I had been grateful just to offload on Veronique, she had listened and been proactive. Using her large network she emailed her contacts, providing me with several new contacts to develop.

Coaching has in fact been one of my main coping strategies since Andrew has been away. Coaching was also my introduction to journaling, an exercise I have found immensely helpful and satisfying during the last year. Making time at the end of the day to record events, feelings etc, is not only a healthy outlet for emotions, it will also serve as a reminder of all you do and achieve, a therapeutic pat on the back.

A pause for reflection:

Early into my experience as the 'stay-at-home' partner I had to do some serious re-evaluation. Rather than sitting back and mourning the loss of our expatriate status and life, I asked myself some questions. What ingredients had there been in expatriate life which had made it such a stimulating and exciting experience for our family? Why should being back in our home country make it so different? Having acknowledged that we were experiencing the normal traumas of repatriation, then came the stark realisation that the main reasons for this imbalance was the prolonged absence of a Dad. We were also missing the familiarity, support and empathy of the normal expatriate support network.

Role models:

Knowing I was the only one to pull us out of this low trough we were experiencing, I scoured local papers and websites for contacts and details of clubs and activities locally which might be of interest to the children. During our time overseas they had always had a variety of hobbies and this was a good springboard. Once these activities had been identified, it was easier. We all felt a bit more on home ground, the kids' interest was re-ignited, because they had a regular activity which interested them, sport. The opportunity to socialise with their peers and have a role model in their individual club leaders was a big step forward. It also meant that by taking the kids to their activities I was beginning to establish a familiar routine and meet other parents.

This was especially important for James, then in his early teenage years and Dad away. His young Takwondo coach was a great role model, respected, enthusiastic, motivated, disciplined, challenging and fun, whilst also supportive. This enthusiasm and motivation was contagious. It gave James focus and challenge and I knew if there were some difficulties he was experiencing which he didn't want to discuss with me, he would talk to his coach about them.

Goal setting:

When you are alone at home, it is very easy to become insular and unsociable and just operate in your little bubble. This is when you need that extra focus and to start setting yourself new goals. Easier said than done you may be thinking, when all you really feel like doing at the end of the day/week, having dealt single handed with everything, is to sit at home and crash in front of the television.

To stay in, you don't have to make an effort, make plans, dress up, or talk to anyone. You have always got the cat for company. Staying in is the easy option, you feel safe and comfortable. You may feel uncomfortable going out alone. To start with, focus on something which is not too high powered, that really interests you and is in a non-threatening environment. It could be signing up for a yoga class, or a local environmental campaign. Next find out the times and dates of the next meeting and diarise. You have just set your first goal: the commitment to attend the meeting.

A helping hand:

I am a great list maker and terrible procrastinator (this book is testament to that) and personally I find it more beneficial to break down my goals into a set of small steps. That way I can tick things off my list, am more proactive and actually enjoy the whole process of achieving my aims.

A good example of this happened several months ago when returning home full of enthusiasm, inspired after a 2-day coaching course with Zoe Meyer. To help extend my local network Zoe's advice had been: research local business networks and attend some of their next sessions. With this in mind, talking to a friend shortly afterwards I discovered that apart from running a local personal development company, Vanessa is also chair of the newest Business Networking Chapter in the area. Before I knew it I had my invitation. She was discerning and intuitive, suspecting that I would probably take it no further. She discovered my agenda however, and by the end of our conversation also had my commitment that I would be at the next breakfast networking session at 6.45 am.

It is much easier to help others make decisions, rather than focus on your own and as the 'stay-at-home' partner you get so used to making decisions on behalf of the family, that it is very easy to consign your own wishes to the bottom of the pile. My discovery was that the only way of ensuring my static written list of goals became a dynamic reality was to encourage and respond to outside input.

Discover your confidence:

It is rather a question of habit, as when a colleague enquired three years ago if I was attending the W.I.N. 2003 (Women's International Networking Conference) in Lausanne, Switzerland. My immediate response was to cite the reasons I could not go, cost, organising cover for the kids and many other negative reasons. However, I was neatly presented with a 'fait accompli' when my husband gave me the cheque for the trip and my mother offered to come up and run the house in my absence.

Being thrown into an unknown situation whetted my appetite. And sure enough during the course of the conference I met fascinating people, many of whom have since become an important part of my network of contacts.

It was fortunate the Conference ran over four days as for the first twenty four hours I was simply in a daze. Thrust into a totally alien environment, all the other participants seeming totally self-assured, professional and at ease, my instinctive reaction was to run for the door. This situation bore the hallmarks of feelings I had experienced during the early days of a new overseas postings: clammy hands, tongue-tied, feeling as though 'new kid on the block' was indelibly tattooed on my forehead. I quickly re-composed myself, though, gathering my shreds of confidence and took the plunge, finding a group and introduced myself.

Only once I had overcome the initial trepidation of breaking into unknown territory and started networking did I realise that the feelings of inadequacy and fear I was experiencing were not unique to me, but shared by many there. It was just our situations that were different. Some were launching themselves in new careers, others were 'empty nesters' enjoying new-found independence and some had no fixed agenda, being just there to enjoy the experience.

There was no looking back. Caution took a back seat and feeling hugely energised, I threw myself into the experience and had a memorable time. Having the opportunity to meet such a variety of people was astonishing: re-connecting with other expatriates, listening to people's dreams and attending a diverse spectrum of workshops was exciting. I learnt how to write a mission statement of my own, maximise my learning potential and grow my own global network. This was a crucial turning point for me and I returned home energised and motivated, ready to start researching material for my book on single-status assignments.

Re-invent yourself:

Being the 'stay-at-home' partner is a good opportunity to reinvent yourself career-wise and I have really enjoyed the diversity these opportunities have offered me.

I had been so encouraged and motivated by the coaching sessions I received from Gail Macindoe, I signed up for two distance learning courses in Life and Business Performance coaching, adding another dimension to my skills portfolio.

Are you ready for a change?

Having worked from home for several years, I was becoming restless though and ready for another change. Knowing that I needed more people contact I worked part-time in a local estate agent and this added several valuable skills to my CV, as well as giving me a healthy break from solitary working. The change of environment not only re-energised me it also increased my motivation level, enabling me to complete researching and writing this book. In fact since then I have moved on and even started exploring other exciting opportunities.

Dual career specialist and well known author of 'Career-in-your-suitcase' Jo Parfitt says: 'I am a firm believer in the power of turning problems into opportunities. While one person may consider being the 'stay-at-home' increases your responsibilities while clipping your wings, another may see this period of enforced time at home as the chance to do some self-development work. Think of all the books you could read about finding your passion or discovering what you could do next with your career? And all those courses you could do on subjects you may never have considered before, from plumbing to reflexology, one of them could fire your enthusiasm. This time alone provides the ideal place from which you can reflect and consider your options carefully. It is a time to explore and a time to focus on learning, networking and building. Enjoy it.'

For those 'stay-at-home' partner who do not face a prolonged break in their careers this continuity aspect delivers considerable health benefits, whilst also offering the considerable advantage of a ready-made support network and social life provided through work. In addition, by stepping out of the home environment and meeting people on a regular basis, they will be less likely to suffer from loneliness and isolation.

Working from home undoubtedly offers much-needed flexibility at certain stages of family life. It can be organised around family demands and responsibilities and the new technology offers a multitude of new ways to work and build a career. But a strategy for getting out and mixing regularly also has to be in place to avoid mental strain.

Each support network is individual and important:

With children at different ages and stages, elderly parents to care for, or career issues to balance, each family's support network needs are inevitably very individual to their situation. Support networks should not be restricted to organised meetings, but viewed more holistically. A visit to an art gallery, a trip to the theatre, walking the dog, a visit to the hairdresser, meeting a friend, or even perhaps a visit to the doctor. All will form part of your support network. Every 'stay-at-homes' support network is unique, fulfilling different criteria. Balancing is the buzzword.

One 'stay-at-home' partner reports that she has begun full-time studying in her partner's absence. She finds it a positive step, building on her current qualifications, and giving herself another interest to focus on, rather than just the family. She says: 'The only drawback I do find is because I am home alone I do not have much time to work uninterrupted.' Another 'stay at home' partner told me that being an active churchgoer had really helped her family's adjustment in the early days of her partner starting short term working. As pre-assignment the family were already enjoying strong support through their local church network, this made the lifestyle transition that much easier.

PART THREE

Researching and Creating Your Own Network

Introduction:

There are many different types of network you can build. The beauty of the support system is that the benefits are reciprocal. Whilst it serves as either professional support or emotional nourishment, you can always return the favour, albeit at a later date.

Get creative:

Create your own network: It is an exhilarating process and even easier with online communication now so prevalent. Useful sources of local information will be local and regional papers, libraries, and the internet. This method of researching will quickly acquaint you with contact opportunities available in your local area, or will serve as a prompt to look further afield to discover what you are truly looking for.

Questions to ask?

Begin by making a checklist to identify your requirements, asking the following questions:

- What sort of support are you looking for the network to provide?
- What sort of people are you hoping to meet?
- How much time can you realistically give to this?
- Will you be able to volunteer your skills?

If there isn't a group in the area of interest to you, start one up by advertising in the local paper, magazine or website.

Don't be shy:

Once you have identified your personal areas of interest, the next step is to begin introductions. One way to break the ice is offer your help either with a function, editing the newsletter, or speaking at the next monthly meeting. Maintaining and updating these networks is vital, the world is transitory, interests change, new people arrive and leave. I found the easiest way to keep my networks, both personal and professional, updated was to record and file details in small file boxes and update weekly onto my database.

Contact local professional women's networking groups, as they often organise breakfast or evening meetings. In the early days of our return I was invited to the Open Day of a ladies networking group which was updating its image. Well organised with taster sessions from various members and local businesses, short talks and lots of networking was a good introduction to my local area. Although not a member, I am on their mailing list, and receive their regular newsletter, this enables me to attend any sessions which interest me, I just pay a guest fee to attend.

It was through this networking group that I was introduced to Vanessa Cobb, who had her own personal development company, Iridica based in Exeter. Vanessa's help over the last two years has been varied. It has included helping me prepare for workshops, practise with public speaking, as well as providing valuable feedback for this book.

These networking groups are a foundation of support, efficient and valuable providers of local knowledge and contacts. Remember networking is effective if you do it daily. The success of any networking lies in its simplicity. You can begin your own local network by a mere introduction to your neighbour, meeting other Mums at the school gate, or offering to do voluntary work at the local school/hospital/conservation project.

One mother with five years experience of short term assignment working says: 'I have a huge self-belief. I have always found it really beneficial to take on voluntary duties, as this helps my self esteem and gets me out meeting different people, adding much needed routine to my week'.

The key to this whole chapter is in simply asking questions. Whether you are invited to a new group or need to ask a favour, once you have asked the question, it will open all sorts of interesting doors. But be warned this is an organic process and will evolve accordingly. There will be some areas which will not interest you; the tip is not to get disheartened. Keep looking, you will find your interest and wonder why it took you so long.

Advice from the expert:

Author of 'Grow your own Network', Jo Parfitt says: 'Regardless of whether you find yourself in a brand new community with your family in tow or in a familiar community without your partner, you need support. Whether that support comes in the form of a cleaner or babysitter, or simply someone to talk to no-one can totally avoid the need for a network. Networking is not just for professionals. Being at home alone can be lonely and it is easy to feel vulnerable when you are solely responsible for day to day living. It is vital that you make an effort to get to know people, lots of people, and fast.'

SUPPORT NETWORK EXERCISES

Pre assignment support:
- Make a list of the people who were part of your support network before short-term assignments became a part of your lifestyle.
- How did they support you?
- Was your support network adequate?

Now your partner is doing short term work. Do you need a different support network?
- Identify your current support network and ways it supports you?
- Where will you find the support you need locally?
- Do you know anyone locally in similar circumstances to yourself?

What do you need the network for?
- Identify the area where you will benefit most from support? Family/Emotional/Professional/Social.
- Do you want to meet people?
- Do you need exercise? Do you like team sports?
- What interests do you have? Walking, canoeing, writing?
- Do you need help with a car share for children's activities?
- Do you need a babysitter?
- Do you need a network to help support your career?

Establishing a network:
- List five things you have found out about groups locally?
- Identify three new networks/groups which interest you.
- Diarise the next meeting to attend.
- How will you practise introducing yourself when you first go to a new network or club?
- What do you want from your new network?

Keeping your network:
- Identify four people you need to get to know.
- How can they support you?
- List two people from the list you will call in the next week.
- List one person you will meet in the next week for coffee/lunch.
- Identify five skills you have which may be helpful to your new network.
- Identify two skills you need to develop to assist your new network.

PART FOUR
Coping Strategies and Helpful Hints

What social life?

When your partner is away and you are restricted by childcare and home responsibilities, going out for an evening can become onerous. Because you are effectively single, invitations to join other couples for evening outings to the theatre and restaurants may dry up. In addition, being on your own you may be unfairly viewed by others as a threat.

Group activities:

It is healthy to recognise that things will not stay the same when your partner starts short-term work and imperative you vary your routine by organising a regular evening out. Evening classes are always a good starting point: join a language class, amateur dramatic club or yoga session. It not only gets you out of the house, but makes you network and socialise with others sharing similar interests. Unlike expatriate life where weekends are casual, relaxed and social, in England weekends are family-orientated and this is again one area we found difficult, just our little unit of three. Today quite a few of my friends are single parents, but most have family living locally and benefit from that support network.

Be flexible and have lots of coping strategies:

My coping strategies have again been severely challenged recently. Both children have moved onto the next chapters of their lives, leaving home within a week of each other. Our sixteen year old daughter Laura, went off to boarding school and James, eighteen, to University. With no previous boarding experience Laura was eagerly anticipating the new experience. Having been at boarding school myself I knew that the first term and total change in her lifestyle would be challenging for her. I also knew how important it was to Laura's settling process that I was upbeat, supportive and not reactive when she phoned home. Being at a distance was difficult, but talking to her practical, well experienced and intuitive house parent and knowing that someone knew she was feeling unsettled and would keep a weather eye on her, lessened my worry.

During that term I also visited Andrew in his new posting for a week. It was lovely to see him and spend a bit of time together. The trip had involved a lot of travelling and socialising. On my return I felt tired and emotional. Thinking it was just the emotional impact of recent events, I was surprised and relieved when the doctor advised my symptoms were probably menopausal. I had been so busy coping with the family's emotional health, I had disregarded my own! Giving emotional support to the rest of the family is important, but can also be draining. It is important that you also look after your own health.

The empty nest:

Constantly programmed to practical mode was a boon for the amount of organisation and retail therapy which pre-empted my kids' departure. The flip side, though, was that being so fixated on the practical I was not prepared for the emotional void after they had left. Only on the return journeys from school and University did the emotional impact hit and the tears start.

The sudden switch from having been pivotal to their lives to experiencing empty nest syndrome, in one fell swoop has been difficult. It is healthy and important to recognise that as young adults they have to start making their own decisions, yet it is probably harder on the 'stay-at-home' partner than the child. With your partner away, you have been so used to making all of the decisions that you can suddenly be left feeling totally redundant. Having a few projects simmering in the background has been immensely useful and helped me focus on other things, such as this book rather than weeping in an empty, clean and strangely quiet house.

A gentle warning:

A word of caution, when you are the 'stay-at-home' partner there is a temptation to offload and rely more on the children. Inadvertently I was doing this, until I was jolted out of it by James, then aged sixteen, who angrily remarked: 'You are being unfair, I am not Dad, I can't handle all this responsibility'. I realised, as the eldest, he had unconsciously been trying to emulate his father's role and take some of the pressure off me. Unfairly and naively I had used our chats as opportunities for offloading day-to-day stuff I would normally have chatted to Andrew about.

Engulfed by a huge wave of guilt, I made a conscious move to change the situation. I realised one simple adjustment I could make was to expand my network further. I joined an afternoon class to improve my French, arranged to meet friends more regularly and began to view my support network in a different perspective.

The sky is the limit:

The beauty of the support network is there are no limits. It can range from helping out a friend with childcare arrangements, offering to take a neighbour shopping, joining a squash club, enrolling in a language class, learning to meditate, employing a career coach, meeting a friend for lunch or doing a degree in anthropology. In creating and maintaining this network, the benefits are far-reaching and you can tailor them to your own requirements and budget. We all need time out, support, friendship and to maybe develop hidden talents. A great way to help you maintain a healthier balance on the home front!

Think big:

View your support network holistically: it should include everything and everyone involved in helping to keep your life more balanced. My own support network includes doctors, dentists, complementary therapists, professional groups, friends, school, family, sports club, gardener. The list is endless. Being able to see this list of different people and resources as your virtual team does wonders to strengthen you in your daily life. Do not limit it to only to those you see regularly around you. I soon discovered I also have a wonderful online support network, which grows daily. The support and friendship I have received whilst researching and writing this book has been fabulous. Contacts, opinions and expertise have been freely and willingly given, with no thought of financial recompense. I believe this is a prime example of the importance of a support network in both your personal and professional life.

A positive process:

The process of embracing the support network concept wholeheartedly has proved wonderfully supportive and calming. Remember you have to be the one prepared to make the effort and go the extra mile. Otherwise you will find yourself unfocused, stuck in the old routine, not enjoying life. Whilst this lifestyle is not ideal, it does not need to be restrictive.

Seize the positive opportunities; you will then be better prepared to deal with negative issues as they happen. It is not enough to plan your family's life around your partner's next visit home; you are living in the here and now and need to design your life accordingly. As John Lennon said ' life is what happens when you are busy making other plans'.

Supporting at a distance:

Knowing that the 'stay-at-home' partner has a supportive network is crucially important for the one actually on the assignment. By their very short term nature, often in difficult, inaccessible locations, local supportive networks do not feature highly on the corporate agenda. Often you will be the only person your partner can offload to. Home office support may be lacking, difficult contractual issues will occur.

This proved to be the case during one of Andrew's assignments. He was the only expatriate on the project with no local office support, very limited home office support and nothing in the way of social facilities. This lack of colleagues to support him made a difficult project, hugely tedious and frustrating. His only escapes were his weekly phone calls home. It was a stressful and unhappy period of time. 'The project' became our main topic of conversation, leaving me with slight lingering resentment that work overlapped so much into all aspects of our lives.

From my own experience as the 'stay-at-home' partner I understood only too well how necessary a good support network was. The project was due to run for another six months, during which time I knew the situation would not change. As our phone calls were the only practical support I could offer, I tried putting myself in Andrew's position.

The phone calls were his highlight, so I ensured that we kept them as upbeat as possible. Focusing on positive things which had happened during the week and developing good listening skills helped. Organising a quick visit to him in posting helped relieve a difficult situation. Seeing the difficulties first hand gave me an overall perspective and helped my understanding. Participating in and seeing his environment helped me empathise more with his situation. Having some knowledge of the location meant I could visualise people and places he would refer to. Maybe a slightly surreal scenario, but I know this change of perspective really helped Andrew's coping abilities whilst he was away. At the time I felt angry, irritated by the company's ambivalent attitude. Here I was not only supporting on the home front, but also taking on the company's problems and I was not even an engineer.

Andrew told me that in his last project, the poor local office support combined with slack home office support impacted hugely on him. He said: 'I ended up shouldering total responsibility for the project. Not being able to share and offload technical project difficulties was especially difficult. The only way of coping was to be totally work-orientated. In order to keep on top of things, I shut everything else out and drove myself hard'.

This approach to coping with such problems can lead to overload. Andrew explained: 'my only time off was ten days every three months when I went home. Lack of company support made the situation doubly difficult. Psychologically, with no family to offload to and relax with, breaking the monotony of work, it was easy to become introverted and insular. I did offload to Marian, who was understanding and enabled me to moan, but I also needed technical support. Organisations sometimes operate an out of sight out of mind mentality, and the assignee becomes an invisible figure. I coped by switching off and just totally concentrated on the assignment. Of course, it impacted on home life, conversation revolved solely around work. It was a difficult time, straining loyalties. Our lives were driven by completely different agendas and never seemed to meet half-way. Marian's life was driven by family and home responsibilities and mine was driven by work. Keeping things balanced called for intuition and understanding all round.'

These situations and frustrations are by no means unusual and will, I am sure, be causing you to nod in agreement as you read this. They could, however, easily be avoided if companies used some foresight and provided adequate preparation pre-assignment' for assignee and the 'stay-at-home' family.

A mother of three, experiencing a very similar situation, told me: 'I have had no support from the company, not even a phone call or letter. I have found the only way of coping is to go on autopilot. I am always trying to problemsolve. It is as though I am constantly acting. The worst part is I feel riddled with guilt because I have to maintain this façade'.

Now on a new posting, the difference in Andrew is immense. Working with several other expatriate colleagues, he is able to talk difficulties through as they occur and also socialise more. The local office support is fantastic and the home office support intuitive and responsible. All of this, combined with our recent introduction to hooking up with Skype, has made a huge difference. His calls to us are more upbeat and less stressed, talking daily over the internet gives everyone the opportunity to chat about day-to-day happenings rather than saving it up for the ten minute weekly phone call.

My personal experience and research illustrates there is a real need for Corporates to re-evaluate their roles and responsibilities within the short term assignment scenario. Corporates would be well advised to discuss and evaluate in-depth the quality and availability of local and home office support. This would be extremely reassuring to all parties. It tells the assignee that he will not be doing it alone and the stay at home can relax guard a little, knowing that there is a framework of a support network.

Feedback:

In hindsight, I should have worked harder during the early days of our repatriation, particularly at building up a bigger support network locally. I was in close contact by phone and email with friends overseas, who lived the expatriate lifestyle, but didn't know anyone living a similar experience locally. It would have been very helpful meeting someone, talking face to face about the highs and lows and would have lessened the isolation I felt.

Family Feedback:

Without the support and contributions of my family, however, this project would never have got past the idea stage. Andrew and both kids have proved willing and enthusiast candidates for my research. By freely sharing their thoughts, emotions and coping strategies with me, they have not only helped me with my writing but strengthened our family relationship. Meeting regularly for frank family discussions has been educational, thought-provoking and at times tempestuous, but also demonstrated that as well as relying and supporting each other, we are learning to be more intuitive. It has made us more respectful and aware of the individual, showing that we are all coping with the experience in different ways.

Well used to my questions and constant search for material, my teenagers shared some of their thoughts with me. Laura then aged fifteen said: 'None of my friends' Dads were working away, so they couldn't fully empathise. Our lifestyle was quite alien to them. My main coping strategy was through sport. I really enjoy hockey and kayaking and always kept busy with after school/weekend kayaking and hockey activities. Being out in the fresh air and doing lots of exercise was motivating and energising. It was my way of offloading and helped me cope better.'
James said: 'Because I was at boarding school, my main support network were my friends and house-parents. What I found really helped was that several of my friends had experience of parents either living overseas or being in the armed forces, so they could empathise and talk about some of the difficulties we experienced. Life at boarding school was always busy, so you didn't have too much time to think. Being in the second year of the Sixth Form, there was quite a lot to think about and important choices to make, Matron and the housemaster were a good background support, giving us lots of useful advice, as well as superb pastoral care.'

Undoubtedly children whose parents are involved with short-term assignment working do become more independent. But because you are the only parent on the front line they will need both practical and emotional support far more intensely than if Dad were at home all of the time. It is fair to say, if you as the 'stay-at-home' are totally exhausted with the practicalities of coping alone, you won't be the most responsive and sympathetic audience when your children come to you with their problems. This is one of the main reasons it is so important the stay-at-home is motivated and proactive in building a nurturing and supportive network.

QUICK TIPS

- Make time to develop a contact within your partner's corporation, in case of emergency.
- Find out whether it has specific policies to support the family.
- Carry out some research on the kind of company help you may be entitled to.
- Evaluate what sort of support networks suits your family.
- Evaluate the type of support you need, friend, hobby, counsellor?
- Network with other 'stay-at home' partners - set up a support group.
- Organise family outings at weekends.
- Arrange regular times to sit and talk frankly as a family.
- Look after your family's health and exercise.
- Build good relationships with school, doctor, local community.
- Join a gym or sports club.
- Do some research on local networks and attend a few meetings to see which ones suit you.
- Do something different, challenge yourself.
- If there is no network start one.
- Join an evening class, learn a language, join a group.
- Make sure you arrange 'time out for you'.
- Organise after-school activities with good role models.
- Research the new technology available and use it, to make life easier.
- Talk regularly with your partner.
- Use family/friend contacts for help with the children, overnight stays

CHAPTER TWO

Relationships and Communications

Introduction:

Working at keeping up regular and good quality communication is essential. It not only helps both parties talk about what they have on their mind, but also keeps the absent partner in the picture about what is happening on the home front. In the long run it also makes the returning home process easier, whilst also helping to maintain a presence in family life, even if virtually and over great distances.

Communicating regularly it helps keep the balance:

The short-term assignment lifestyle has enormously benefited from modern technology. In fact it has completely changed many aspects. Use of email, webcam and video phones provides an efficient and economic mode of communication. It enables the family to stay in more regular contact with the assignee who feels more 'in touch' with his family's daily routine. It is brilliant for interacting (albeit virtually) with younger children by reading bedtime stories, or just chatting and catching up with their partner and older children's activities, progress at school, etc.

Lois Bushong, a licensed marriage and family therapist at Eagle Creek Counselling in Indianapolis, Indiana explained: 'There needs to be regular contact, daily if at all possible, via cell phone or email. This contact needs to be more than a report of what the kids are doing and what bill was due that day. If they can, think back to those many hours of long phone calls when they were dating and return to those types of discussions. They need to check in with each other emotionally, talk about a book they are both reading, plan what they are going to do when they see each other, dream of the future over the phone.'

Skype and Email contact:

Everyone I talked to admitted that improved convenience and efficiency of email, msn, Skype and the mobile phone was a major boon. It made their partners' absence more bearable, as well as helping contribute to the smoother running of life on the home front.

The convenience of email communication has proved a vital tool to our own family during Andrew's absence abroad. If I was having a bad day, one of my favourite coping strategies was to sit at the computer and type frantically for a while. Having this opportunity to instantly offload was incredibly therapeutic, some mails didn't even get sent, staying in my draft box for deletion at a later date. Like me, James has always been an avid fan of emailing. Regular use of email contact with his Dad did in fact help develop a new dimension to their relationship. Even if Dad was at a distance it helped strengthen their father/son bond. It not only kept Dad updated on daily routine, it gave James another outlet to air any worries which he may have.

Laura who preferred telephone contact with her Dad explained: 'Although it was helpful having regular email contact, I always found it boring. I preferred to phone Dad, even if it was only a short conversation, I could always say much more than in an email. It helped to keep Dad updated with our lives, I really enjoyed speaking to him, it used to make him feel nearer.'

Balancing relationships is perhaps one of the most difficult aspects of this lifestyle. Whilst I am a practical, straightforward person and could well recognise the many benefits of internet/mobile technology which supported and sustained family and individual relationships, it was also invasive. Using email/Skype helped us update each other with what was going on in our daily lives, but it also had its own disadvantages. Whilst the use of Skype allows the absent partner to be more interactive with the family at home, this can be deceptive. You are indeed able to talk things through in detail, but the reality is that that you are still separated by distance and it falls to you to make the major decisions unsupported.

In my experience, the difficulty was that I wrote/talked about current domestic/family issues which were important at the time. What had seemed an insurmountable problem one day was soon replaced by another equally important domestic issue. If you are not careful it can create a tendency for the 'stay-at-home' partner to try and keep the absent partner continually updated. This in my experience is not only impractical but also impossible. I tried this and it wasn't long before I felt overwhelmed, as though I was on an electronic lead.

It was the surreal situation most 'stay-at-home' partners constantly struggle with. Yes, the benefits of modern communication are huge, but with these improvements come disadvantages. We had always emailed regularly and then there was Skype, 24/7 online communication and it was a steep learning curve. Knowing that I could talk at the click of a button, I found myself calling Andrew discussing minutae. Things which in the past I had taken and dealt with in my stride, suddenly necessitated microscopic evaluation. I was fast losing confidence.

One 'stay-at-home' partner commented: 'Although email is great for telling each other about our lives, I like to hear a voice. There are simply things I do not feel comfortable with putting in writing. You can't gauge reactions or explain if the other person does not understand.'

Let the technology work for you:

For me one of the main challenges and excitements of living the short term assignment lifestyle is becoming the major decision maker. Having the responsibility to make informed and important decisions unsupported had always been my job. The trick is not to become a slave to the technology, develop a programme of contact which works best for you. Early morning contact always worked much better for me, when I was in a more relaxed frame of mind and had time. It is detrimental to your relationship if maintaining regularity of communication becomes your prime motivator, rather than the quality of communication. The best advice is to stand back, identify the benefits of particular technology to your individual families' requirements, devise a programme of use and let the technology work for you.

As the 'stay-at-home' partner, I was so used to dealing with everything and everyone; it was very easy to become short-sighted and controlling. It is much harder to let go. One of my major difficulties was acknowledging that my way wasn't the only way. I was so used to coping and fielding the daily responsibilities that I didn't need anybody else's opinion or input. I became quite territorial and resentful if Andrew and I started discussing the children. What did he know? He wasn't dealing with all the emotions involved, thousands of miles away. The family were just distorted voices over the phone line.

I asked the Director of the Southern California based Center for the Study of Long Distance Relationships and author of 'Long Distance Relationships', Dr Greg Guldner, for his thoughts on the long and short term effects a parent's absence has on the development of the children. He explained: 'In general the effect of absence on a child seems to depend on the response of the individual who stays with the children. When the parents view the separation as a crisis or are negatively affected then the child seems to have (at least short term) difficulties coping. There are not many studies on this from the civilian standpoint but from the military, which has done several. A useful resource is www.cfs.purdue.edu/mfri which is the Military Family Research Institute.'

Learning to share:

I was frankly a bit jealous of my role as the pivotal person in the children's daily lives. We were a close unit and they should be able to talk to me about everything, I thought. Realising that whilst I was the only parent on the ground I was not indispensable proved a timely but rude awakening. I made a conscious effort, stepped back and re-evaluated. I came to recognise that each parent's contribution, opinion etc was equally important in helping keep family relationships happy, sustained and balanced. Rather than as in the past, continually viewing things from my perspective, I deliberately slowed down, and really started listening to the kids. This helped me gain more understanding of different difficulties they were encountering linked with Andrew's absence and slowly a healthier more comfortable family relationship evolved.

How long are you home for?

This is dependant on the type of industry your partner works for. The oil and gas industry, for instance, is well known for assignees working in rotation, away for several months and then having a chunk of time 'at home'.

In our own family's experience, leave periods for less than a week definitely did not work. When Andrew returned more regularly, but for shorter periods of time, it caused conflict because time was not on our side and there was an underlying stress. It took time for everyone to adjust to him being at home and then, just as we had adjusted, the dynamics changed and he was off again. It was quite disruptive to home life and something we now try to avoid. Through your own personal experience and talking it through together, you will find the most satisfactory arrangement for your own family.

One 'stay-at-home' mother of three, whose partner returns one week out of five, told me: "He cannot fit in very well with my routine and things are rather chaotic for a week. I look forward to seeing him and am rather glad to see him go!'

When asked what effect the short term assignment has had on her marriage, one veteran 'stay-at-home' partner candidly told me: 'We found it a big strain, never enough time when he was home to fully catch up. The stress on both sides caused arguments and resentfulness.'

There doesn't seem to be a happy medium. It would appear that opting for longer periods of work away from home is preferable, as it gives everyone in the family the benefit of spending prolonged quality time together and helps make the assignee's re-entry and integration back into family life easier. Extended time at home is far more realistic, revealing the cracks in family life which can then be addressed. They could otherwise easily be forgotten amongst the many other demands of short-term assignment work.

Whilst shorter and more frequent trips home can ensure continuity of the assignee's presence within the family, most 'stay-at-homes' agree that it is disruptive, as one comment underlined: 'My husband did a seven month project and came home every six weeks. Frankly this was a disaster and very uncomfortable. The whole family suffered and we vowed not to do it again. My husband was either jetlagged and tired or packing to go again!'

When I asked marriage and family therapist, Lois Bushong for her views on the maximum assignment length she would recommend for a married couple, she replied: 'It is all so dependent on the emotional health of the couple, the age of the children and the support system of the family that is left behind. There are so many variables. I would generally say that if an absence is going to be longer than a month, the couple needs to seriously look at how often they are going to do this, the developmental stages of their children and how they might maximize their couple times and creatively carve out time together.'

What do you tell them?

Given the distances involved, you tend to be circumspect about what you divulge to the working partner. Well aware that to regale them with every domestic crisis is a definite no-no, you have to trust your intuition and just get on with things. It is hardly surprising that in these circumstances the 'stay-at-home' partner becomes more independent and self-reliant, adept at playing Jekyll and Hyde.

One 'stay-at-home' partner said: 'I think we tend to keep bad news from each other. In some respects we are both so terribly independent that we only share good news when we are together'.

What do you miss?

'I guess what I am saying is I miss all the little stuff, a hand to hold, someone to share a cup of tea with, making dinner together, talking about a news programme', admitted one 'stay-at-home' partner.

Re-entry and the cutlery drawer scenario:

In the early days of Andrew's short term working experiences, one of my main annoyances was that on returning home he would immediately go to the kitchen and start re-organising the cutlery drawer. This was not the best start to home leave. I saw it as a threat, an invasion of my position and space and he couldn't see the problem! Filing it away as one of those quirky, unexplained things men do, I was reassured to read expatriate author Robin Pascoe's latest book for expatriates, 'Raising Global Nomads - parenting abroad in an on demand world' and her apt advice for returning assignees: '…when you come home from a business trip, don't feel you have to immediately reintegrate yourself into the family and your spouse's good books by re-arranging the cutlery drawer. I can't count how many women have told me that this particular action (is there a cutlery fetish that has gone unreported?) was the straw that broke their own exhausted backs.'

Now that I realise this was one of his coping strategies in dealing with re-entry to the family, I am more understanding and it has ceased to be such an irritant.

Giving time out:

Whatever the type of short-term assignment your partner is employed on, it goes without saying they will return tired from the intensity of the project and jet lagged from the constant travel and different time zones. Diplomacy is the name of the game and needs practice. It is highly recommended that you do not greet your partner at the front door with a list of DIY chores. For all concerned there needs to be an agreed 'switch-off time'. In our experience the twenty four hour rule worked really well. It was an unwritten family rule, the first twenty four hours Andrew was back, we left him to his own devices. That period of time was necessary for his re-adjustment to family life after an absence of several months. Every family is different and will discover 'a switch off time' that works for them.

Constant re-adjustment:

As I previously mentioned, the key to successfully maintaining this long-distance lifestyle is awareness of the constant need for flexibility and balance. This type of work places huge strains on all relationships. From the 'stay- at- home' partner's perspective, resentments can occur and build up if not addressed. Having to shoulder the relentless daily responsibilities of family, home and work, only punctuated on an irregular basis with short visits from the assignee, makes maintaining the balance difficult. Your confidence and self-esteem take a battering. One of the difficulties many find it hard to cope with is that your own real life is often put on hold, whilst the assignee is back.

Everyone is acutely aware that time together is limited and precious, so more emphasis is placed on having a nice time, resulting in a façade of artificiality, leaving no time to explore and experience the ups-and-downs which are an integral part of family and home life.

One 'stay-at-home' partner commented: 'I have a tendency to want our time together to be perfect, so I don't say anything about the petty annoyances that crop up between two people.'

Are you prepared?

My own research clearly revealed that if the 'stay-at-home' partners and their families had received some form of pre-assignment briefing from their companies, similar to location briefings expatriates receive before going on assignment, it would have made things easier and help avoid many problems. 'It would have been nice to have had some benchmark to measure experiences by. It would have given me confidence and I would have been prepared and better equipped to deal with the difficulties as they occurred, rather than constantly fumbling my way in the dark', commented one American 'stay-at-home' partner. Marriage and family therapist, Lois Bushong said: 'It might be helpful if pre-assignment companies offered couples the opportunity of some form of professional psychological testing such as those tests that tell us their marital satisfaction, their own emotional health'. She continued: 'Basically if the relationship is fragile in any way, short term assignment working is not for you.'

Questions to be considered pre-assignment

Company support:

- How many home trips would your partner make? Who would pay for these trips?
- What type of information/resources have you received from the company?
- Do the company offer you a paid trip to visit in posting?
- Have the company offered some pre-assignment training to you and your partner?
- What support/benefits have the company offered in your partner's absence?
- What company support would help you?
- Have you been provided with a contact within the company?
- Do you know any contacts with experience of this lifestyle that could help advise you?

Your family relationship:

- What distance could you cope with if your partner was working away?
- What duration do you envisage your partner doing short term work for?
- Is your partner very pro-active with home responsibilities?
- What difference does your partner's absence make to your relationship/family?
- How do you envisage coping in your partner's absence?
- Have you discussed this as a couple/family?
- How have you decided to share the responsibilities of home/finance?
- Are you practical and independent?
- What are your main worries about embarking on this type of assignment?
- What are your partner's main worries about embarking on this type of assignment?
- What are your children's worries about this type of assignment?
- How have you dealt with these worries?
- Do you sometimes feel depressed?

Your support network:

- Do you have a supportive GP?
- Do you have hobbies?
- Do you have easy email access?

- Do you have finances available for extra help with the house/garden/babysitting?
- Do you have a good support network locally?
- Do you have good childcare available?
- Do you find it easy to meet new people?
- Are you a member of a gym or sports club?

Discuss together the negatives and compromises which will have to be made pre-assignment:

The transitory nature of this lifestyle can cause loneliness and strained personal relationships for all the family. It is vital that the decision to do this type of work is not taken lightly and that both parties are aware of the potential negatives involved. It is naïve to assume that things will not change and a pre-requisite that relationships benefit from some renovation and new objectives pre –assignment, rather than a year down the road.

Organisation and pre-planning for assignee's return leave is essential:

Careful organisation and pre-planning become an integral part of this lifestyle and we have found it useful to prioritise issues before your partner's arrival. Whether it is doing some overdue household maintenance, having a short family holiday or meeting up with friends, we are careful to arrange an agenda for the returning partner's visit which includes input from the children as well. This ensures a healthy variety of activities together and when the departure day looms again, everyone feels they have benefited positively from the visit.

Two years ago, our son James then aged sixteen was due to receive his GCSE results in late August. Six months earlier, whilst planning Andrew's leave, we were careful to prioritise, ensuring that his home leave coincided with the publication of James' results. His return had a dual purpose: not only would it support our son's pre-results jitters, it would also help restore my emotional equilibrium! Having endured five tricky, fragile weeks, supporting, motivating and helping James navigate the exam path Mum was ready for a break and a bit of support. Andrew is a more laid-back character than I and his presence at home lightened the situation, enabling us to put exams on the back burner.

When the dreaded results day dawned, I was anxious, but knowing that Andrew was around at such an important stage of James' academic career was a huge relief. An added plus was being able to celebrate as a family once the results had arrived, which was wonderful.

This summer, with the double whammy of both teenagers expecting exam results, we were experienced and well prepared. They were published over a two week period and so Andrew's summer leave was booked to coincide with the exam results. The pre-planning ensuring that Dad was around at important events in the year was a strategy that always worked really well for us. By recognising and acknowledging the importance of family landmarks throughout the year and planning home leaves around them, we have all benefited. Re-grouping as a family and being able to share these experiences has not only helped strengthen the family bond and been hugely supportive for myself and the kids, it has also definitely reinforced Andrew's position in the family despite his absences.

Organise regular trips home it helps the planning process:

Organising regular visits home are essential. Not only do they provide all parties with a shared objective, they are necessary to the maintenance and nurturing of the whole family relationship. It might mean that you have to finance several trips personally and it is sometimes difficult to look beyond the financial cost. One of the reasons for you doing this type of work is no doubt financial, but it is wise to look beyond the financial implications and empathize with the wider benefits these visits will bring everyone.

The assignee can feel disconnected from home don't be too rigid in your normal routine:

Home leave means different things to different people. Often the assignee is content just to relax and 'be at home' for the duration of his leave, whilst the partner, having experienced long periods coping at home with children, will view these periods as opportunities to socialise and get out and about.

A compromise needs to be reached. Have a plan and be intuitive. If your partner enjoys cooking - and he/she is willing - let him/her take over the responsibility for family meals, giving you time out of the kitchen. Now might be the time to finish that book or write that letter.

Social lives when your partner is back:

It is difficult with your partner away for chunks of time to successfully maintain a social life. In my own experience, when Andrew comes home, he just wants to switch off. He is perfectly content to simply be 'at home'. I on the other hand would view his visits home as a welcome chance to get out together as a couple, away from my normal environment, to re-establish contacts with old friends and re-ignite our social life. This was entirely unrealistic. Social lives, as with all relationships, need nurturing, without which they shrivel up and die. Because it is you who wants and probably needs most the contact, you have to be the initiator keeping up your connections with others.

This is where prioritising, re-evaluation and compromise are good coping strategies. For most 'stay-at-home' partners, keeping the balance within the family relationships is difficult enough without extra responsibilities. If you are not careful, over time this can cause resentment on both sides of the relationship and it is easy to start drifting apart. We compromised; identifying friends we had sporadic contact with and saw irregularly. The core of these friends, were contacts from our expatriate postings that were in fact equally used to and comfortable with the sporadic contact. Arrangements to meet up with these friends were often last minute and unplanned due to changes in Andrew's work commitments. Although not ideal and a bit ragged, we did have some semblance of a social life, ticking a few of the expectation boxes, if not all. Our tendency though was to go out as a family, either for a meal, to the cinema or theatre . This was probably because family time together was so limited and it was the only way we could benefit from his time back 'en famille.'

Encourage teenage children to visit in posting:

This is great for both parties. Not only does it introduce teens to the absent parent in another light, it also gives them the opportunity to see another culture and maybe do some voluntary work. When James was sixteen he visited his Dad who was then working in the Middle East. The trip was a combination of a holiday and a cultural trip. An old overseas contact provided an opportunity for James to spend some of the time doing voluntary work in summer camps, working with Palestinian children from surrounding refugee camps. It gave him valuable 'hands on' experience, added more interest to his CV, and widened his consideration of potential careers, to include working within the humanitarian sector - something he would never have considered before that trip. It is extremely valuable in providing both the parent and child quality time to enjoy each others company, update and build on changing relationships

Worrying and the 'what if's?'

It is only human that at times of insecurity your mind starts playing the 'what if?' game. I spent many fruitless hours worrying about the 'what if's', 'What if another contract didn't materialise? What would we do about finances?' was a constant nagging thought. The more I worried, the more questions materialised until I was totally submerged by these unknowns. It inevitably began to seriously affect my ability to cope with the here and now of keeping everything balanced at home.

The important thing to remember is that whilst healthy to have these thoughts, it is not good to let them fester. Practice optimism. By all means acknowledge the fears, but then put them in a box and get on with your lives. Something will come up, it always does!

Emotions tend to do cartwheels when involved with this lifestyle and there is always uncertainty lurking somewhere! Life plods along satisfactorily for a few months and then the end of the contract looms, further assignments are not evident, enter worry and uncertainty. The trick here is to get things in perspective and have a coping plan.

Children and discipline:

It is inevitable that the 'stay-at-home' partner becomes the major disciplinarian. Your own personal perspective depends entirely on the individual family's situation, but I think it important that the 'stay-at-home' parent retains the more proactive disciplining role, even whilst the expatriate is home. I know from experience that whilst I wanted a break from the parenting during Andrew's brief home leave, there was always the nagging knowledge that these visits should be viewed in positive terms and a disciplining role would spoil this. This was a subject often discussed and we found compromise to be the best course of action. Being the consistent partner at home, I continued to implement the discipline, but we always talked things through and got the other's perspective. It is difficult being the mainstay of the family, traditional roles are impossible to retain when faced with this type of living situation and a lot of role reversal occurs. Communication is the key.

Family and Marriage counsellor, Lois Bushong said: 'The absence of the parent can and many times does impact the bond of the child and the parent, the absent parent at times becomes the 'Santa Claus' parent as they are not there to deal with the discipline issues and don't want to jump into that role if they are there for a few short weeks. So the parent who remains at home becomes the 'bad cop' and the other parent becomes 'Santa Claus' which is very unfortunate. At times all of the anger at the absent parents boils over years later and they have to do a lot of hard work to rebuild that parent-child bond. I feel the children could be more responsible in some areas, helping the 'stay-at-home' parent with the household chores but they struggle in their emotional development.'

The Shhh word – SEX, merely a tick off the 'to do' list?

This subject is not on everyone's agenda for discussion, but is an important part of your relationship and should be acknowledged. The short term assignment lifestyle is not for everyone and can, if they are unprepared, take a toll on partners, both physically and emotionally. One 'stay-at-home' partner with more than five years experience of her husband doing short term assignments, wryly reported that she had began to view sex as another tick off the domestic 'to do' list! Humorous no doubt, but it does give a clear indication of how quickly, the 'stay-at-home' partner can become swamped by family demands.

With the partner away for often long periods, coping alone and being alone become the norm and you can become selfish. As well as investing in some quality 'you time', there is the need to invest in quality 'couple time'.

Marriage counselling:

You may be puzzled, asking why I have put marriage counselling before the sub-heading of marriage breakdown. Surely the natural place for inserting marriage counselling is after the marriage breakdown? I disagree. Most people are so tied into the demands of modern life and so busy living in the moment that they may fail to recognise and acknowledge less immediate difficulties. There will inevitably be issues which have through either personal choice or necessity been relegated to the background. These hovering background issues have a habit of evolving into huge insurmountable problems, if left to fester, unresolved. These can often be avoided if perception and communication are used.

If couples are experiencing marital difficulties, they will often need to look beyond their immediate network for support. Meeting instead with a qualified counsellor or therapists if you are experiencing marriage difficulties whilst your partner is away on a short term assignment, it is doubly difficult. If you and your partner are experiencing individual meltdown, the natural tendency is to withdraw slightly, maybe limiting the communication. The danger is that with both parties physically distanced, the situation becomes fraught with emotion and worry. Things which worked in the past, email and telephone conversations are suddenly no substitute for meaningful and in-depth conversations. Instead things become confrontational and, inevitably, communication eventually stops. Marriage and family counsellor, Lois Bushong said: 'I would suggest that the one who is left behind get into marital counselling even if their spouse is unable to attend. The marriage counsellor can be a wonderful force of specific suggestions that can help them in their own unique situation or challenges. Even if the counselling is with one person it will impact the two of them.'

Your doctor will be happy to recommend a qualified counsellor. Alternatively, the internet or local telephone book is also a good source of contacts. If you are abroad and experiencing marital crisis, your Embassy or International School will often have contact numbers of several recommended and qualified counsellors. Talking to an impartial and intuitive party will help clear the fog of your emotions and help you prepare a foundation, a starting point from which you can move forward into the future. Some companies are pro-active, offering marriage counselling within their support package. However some people will not want their marital problems known to the company. They view their difficulties as failures and prefer to keep them private. Whatever your situation and location there is bound to be some form of supportive advice available, it is up to you whether you take it.

Infidelity:

Interestingly topics such as infidelity and sex are rarely discussed in the short term scenario. Sometimes it goes unacknowledged because people find it too embarrassing. As the aim of this chapter is to explore and encourage frank communication between families and partners, I will get on my metaphorical orange box.

Whilst short term assignment working ticks many of the corporate boxes, the knock-on effects for family and assignee are immense. Working in distant locations, often for long periods, with minimum home and local office support and separated from family and home, it is easy to see how this type of assignment can, if unprepared, impact negatively on a marriage. For many, infidelity reflects an attempt to resolve problems by bringing in a third and unwanted party, the other lover. If spouses are honest with one another's needs, the probability of infidelity is greatly reduced.

Picture the assignee working long hours, feeling rather anonymous, isolated and lonely in a different culture. He will most probably also be living a monotonous hotel/serviced apartment existence with little contact locally and no face-to-face family support. Frequently he feels it is not worth the effort to embrace the expatriate social life because they will only be there for a short time. The result can be a lonely and resentful assignee.

Pressures of work, absence of family support and enforced solitude are all potential catalysts for the partner to start seeking company outside of the marriage. The very nature of short term assignments makes it easy and convenient for both parties to stop working in tandem and begin operating individually. The key to navigating the rough patches is to be aware of the pitfalls and have at the outset implemented a strong, frank and regular agenda for communicating. It will not only help keep you both supported during difficult times, but also preserve and strengthen your relationship.

If your relationship experiences infidelity there will naturally be anger, guilt and resentment felt on both sides. Of vital importance is to keep the channels of communication open. If you are finding it tough talking to your partner about things, get outside help and talk to a marriage guidance counsellor. Just by talking, voicing your anxieties, your resentment and anger, this will be the first step in the healing process. Once you have given yourself permission to talk to someone about the problem, it will become easier. The counsellor might provide you with some tried and tested coping strategies, possibly even an introduction to someone locally who is experiencing similar issues. Talking about the problem with a counsellor will give you both support, clarity and focus, as well as giving your relationship a new foundation to work from.

Marriage breakdown:

For some, short term assignment working has been the final straw which broke the camel's back – their marriage. Over the years the 'stay-at-home' partner has learnt to cope with the strains and demands of coping alone. She/he is independent and has had to carve out a separate life for her/himself, in which her/his partner plays little or no part. The assignee's life is now ruled by travel and the assignment. The bond, the family umbilical cord, which has until recently strengthened the family is now at breaking point.

Everyone is keenly aware of extra responsibilities and has inevitably struggled to cope individually. In the past they would perhaps have sought advice and moral support from Mum, Dad or at least within the family unit. Separated from family by long distances, outside distractions may become attractive and available. With everyone operating autonomously outside of the family, it is easy to see how the family unit can start to slowly disintegrate. With this lifestyle having good communication skills is an absolutely essential tool, which you have to constantly work on at improving. However if you find yourself struggling with your communication skills, it is worthwhile considering taking part in workshops on personal development, presentation and public speaking. This will not only boost both your confidence and social skills, most importantly it will keep you talking.

Substance abuse:

As with marital breakdown substance abuse is often kept under wraps. 'Substance abuse is still a shame-based issue and not a popular subject in polite company' says Connie Moser, an expatriate writer living in the Netherlands. 'For the absent partner lack of family support and homesickness combined with nothing else to do, can make alcohol an attractive alternative. We don't always choose what is good for us we choose what is easiest. There is a need for more provision of counselling services. In Brussels and Holland there is a voluntary organisation (Counselling Europe, www.counsellingeurope.com) of certified therapists, psychiatrists and psychologists specifically experienced to offer advice or counselling. The short term assignment lifestyle can be a lonely experience for both the absent partner and 'stay-at-home' partner. Alcohol and drugs can become coping mechanisms. The trick is rather than relying on alcohol for relaxation, think about pampering yourself, have a bubble bath, read a book, hire a DVD.'

Debt and gambling:

Short term assignments often mean that families incur additional expenses of financing assignee travel and running two separate homes. Whilst the internet is a huge boon providing instant communication and information, it also has its dark side. The internet is a convenient tool; people don't even have to go out of their own homes. Its instant accessibility to on-line gambling can be a temptation and prove addictive. The issues of debt and gambling will, if uncontrolled, prove a strain and drain not only on the family coffers but also on family relationships. I explore the nuances of budgeting and finances in the final chapter but, as pointed out earlier in this one, communicating is the key, whatever the aspect of your relationship experiencing difficulties. It will be helpful to talk it through with someone who is qualified, pro-active and supportive. They can help you make the positive steps to salvage your relationship

Visit your partner in posting it gives you valuable 'couple time':
Explore the possibility of visiting your partner in his posting. It will provide a rare opportunity to have some valuable time together without the demands of home/family. The insight into his work and environment, 'Andrew's difficult project' as we called it, was an excellent vehicle for motivating me to 'take a dose of my own medicine'. Visiting him in posting for a week was, in fact, a real and necessary education for the whole family. I had a true glimpse of the difficulties he encounters on a daily basis.

On my return, having seen the fuller picture, I was much more understanding of his need to 'let off steam' during our regular calls and emails. I became more pro-active in my listening. You get so used to coping alone with your own routine and responsibilities; it is often difficult to look outside the box. The trip helped me realise that I am not the only one who is shouldering huge responsibilities single handed. It has to be a partnership with understanding and independence. Having time together without the demands of family turned out to be rewarding and positive. It gave us the opportunity to talk about the future as well as the day-to-day stuff and just being a couple again was great. I should add that the only way I was able to make this visit a reality was with the invaluable help of my support network.

Writer and careers specialist, Jo Parfitt endorsed the value of these trips to her family when her husband, Ian was doing short term assignment work. She said:

'I did visit Ian when he was in Aberdeen, Gatwick and even The Hague. I did both with the kids and also alone. I thought it was helpful for the children to see where Dad worked and for him to feel that we did not completely disassociate with his other life. However, it was when I went alone that things got exciting. Not being one to hang around in a bed and breakfast or empty flat all day, I would pre-arrange a workshop to run so that I had at least a full day's work planned. I would look up old friends who lived there (they always did) and also try to attend a local networking event.

I thoroughly enjoyed all these trips. Ian could see I was motivated and enthusiastic about my work potential and that gave him hope, I expect, that we might move there one day. I really enjoyed being able to go out in the evenings with him without worrying about children or babysitters and having quality time alone together. What's more, Ian had the chance to introduce me to his colleagues, it let me have an insight into his life and that was good for both of us. The upshot of this is that I loved The Hague so much we did join him!! And we are still there two years later. It was the best thing I ever did.'

Ill health:

Those used to the short-term assignment working patterns often liken the experience to living on a roller coaster. As with long-term expatriate postings, there is the honeymoon phase, the new project arrives in a flurry of activity, excitement and adjustment. Then there is the settling-in and feeling comfortable stage, when everything becomes easier and more familiar. Suddenly the settled feeling is overtaken by the prospect of the end of the contract and there is the repatriation stage to be surmounted. Expatriate life is rather different. It comprises of different transitions: an expatriate experience encompassing the cycle from expatriation to repatriation is often over a period of two years or more. If you squeezed the whole expatriate experience into a six month period only, then you would really begin to understand the intensities involved with short term work and the strains placed on the assignee and family.

Short-term assignment working is very time orientated, often leaving families a very short period in which to discuss the practicalities, let alone the economic realities and vulnerabilities of this lifestyle. In my experience, if these things are not discussed with the assignee face-to-face, there is a tendency for them to be filed in the 'forgotten' file'.

Often these issues demand a quick response; I found the best way to cope in these circumstances was to:

- Pre-arrange a call/email to your partner, ensuring that both parties know the purpose of the call/mail is to be dedicated to dealing with the issue (banking, medical).
- Make a list, prioritising topics for discussion.
- Discuss with partner and prepare an action plan.

The following checklist might also be helpful:

- Do the company request the assignee to have a comprehensive medical pre-assignment? What company support is your partner entitled to if he is taken ill on assignment?
- What are the standards of medical facilities available locally in posting?
- Does the company have a medical emergency procedure? If so what is the procedure?
- Does your partner have adequate insurance cover if his recuperation is lengthy?
- What period of time will the company cover for your partner's absence from the project because of medical problems?
- Is his job safe if he is sick?

Redundancy:

As with ill health, redundancy is often something you cannot be totally prepared for. It is useful to have a general plan of action which you have both discussed, agreed and implemented before starting short-term work. Being prepared ensures that if an emergency occurs, you have a basis to work on.

The following checklist might be helpful:

- What notice period is the assignee entitled to?
- How would the notice period and final payment be effected?
- Do you have a financial reserve to rely on the event of redundancy?
- Will it be enough?
  We were advised by our financial advisors to have a reserve of 3 months salary.
- When was the last time you re-evaluated your reserve? Does it need updating?

One 'stay-at-home' wife with five years experience warns: 'You have to be prepared both personally and financially. This is where the pre-planning is so important, always making allowances for the lean times. When my husband was at home for several months between contracts, we managed on a stricter budget than usual and forgot about our savings. It was a huge period of adjustment, not only was I used to him being away for long periods, but I had been the one in charge of the finances. Suddenly there was a huge shift in the dynamics. It was only by talking things through, making plans and drawing boundaries beforehand that we avoided many potential pitfalls.'

What's on offer?

The need for family support in the context of short-term assignments is now enjoying a higher profile. Companies are slowly realising they need to do more for their employee's family. Currently, whilst some companies are far sighted and do recognise the need for family support - ranging from pre-assignment familiarisation, career coaching, child care allowance and marriage counselling - sadly it is not yet the 'norm'. Don't be shy. Focus on specific areas of support you would find helpful and approach your company with your ideas. They could surprise you!

Listed below is company support received from some of those I researched.

- Tax Advice
- Allowance for internet/mobile phone provision
- Yearly subscription to Global Connections Magazine
- Regular contact with company

Family feedback:

Chatting through our experiences as a family during a recent holiday provoked some interesting reactions:

Andrew said: 'Not being part of daily family life, you can soon feel an outsider. It is important to have individual time together with your children and spouse, it helps re-establish the connection. Time is always at a premium. Though not naturally a talker, since doing short term assignments, I now make a real effort to talk things through at a deeper level and consequently have a better perspective of difficulties they face on the home front.

Much more difficult is the relationship with your spouse. Although we have always emailed daily and talked several times per week, because our relationship is not developing on a daily basis, you very quickly start operating as two individuals, with a very different agenda. It is quite a shock and takes time to get used to each other again. The reality is that just as soon as you feel comfortable with each other, it is time to start packing and travelling again. With long absences and your wife taking on much of the traditional role at home, it is easy to see how couples do start drifting apart. It takes a lot of effort and emotion to keep your relationship balanced and you need a good sense of humour.'

'Stay-at-home' partner Marian says: 'Although we email daily and speak several times per week, it is no substitute for Andrew being here. Knowing your partner is only back for a short period of time, you want it to be a positive experience and enjoy quality time as a family. It can become quite tense with everyone trying too hard and resentment can creep in. You work hard at trying to make it just right, perfect. It is easy for ongoing family issues and responsibilities to take over, but important that both partners make time for each other, plan a weekend away, go for a walk or visit the theatre.'

Sixteen year old Laura said: 'There was no limit to the calls we made to Dad, we didn't take advantage of it but used to phone him when stuff happened with school, exam results etc. I guess when Dad was away, the family relationship was often unbalanced, because it was only Mum and just with three of us, it could be a bit insular. It only took a few days of Dad being home to balance the equation.'

James aged eighteen said: 'I think that if anything it has strengthened our relationship as a family. I appreciate what both mum and dad do for me a lot more. When Dad is away, I feel I don't have someone to talk to on the same level. We are quite alike and share the same sense of humour, I miss bantering with him.'

QUICK TIPS

- Communicate regularly, by phone, e mail, Skype.
  It is important to talk about the daily things
- Don't be intimidated by technology, let it work for you.
- Don't go it alone learn to share family responsibilities with your partner.
- Have a pre-arranged 'time out period' on assignee's return.
- Be prepared for the return and re-adjustment routine:
  'the cutlery drawer scenario'.
- Prioritise what is important, you can't tell them everything.
- Be honest; tell your partner what you miss when he is away.
- Be prepared for the constant re-adjustment.
- How prepared are you for the assignment.
- Do a pre-assignment checklist.
- Discuss negatives and compromises of short term working.
- Important to pre-plan regular trips home for the assignee.
- Pre-plan family trips and activities when the assignee is back to
  ensure family quality time.
- Arrange trips to visit your partner in posting.
- Can teenage children visit in posting?
- Re-evaluate your social life, what works now?
- Regularly re-evaluate personal and family relationships.
- Establish jointly agreed boundaries relating to children, discipline etc.
- If you are having marital problems, seek qualified help.
- Be aware of potential problems, substance abuse, gambling.
- Have you got a plan of action in the event of ill health or redundancy?
- Research your partner's company policy for specific benefits you may be entitled to.

RELATIONSHIPS AND COMMUNICATIONS EXERCISES

Who is important?

- Who are the most important people in your life?
- How important are they?
- Do you regularly tell them how important they are?
- What do you do to support and maintain these important relationships?

How and when do you communicate?

- What sources do you utilize to communicate while your spouse is away:
  Phone, e mail, webcam?
- Is cost of communication covered by company or personal?
- If communicating by phone do you discuss the little happenings of your day?
- Do you keep a list of things to be covered in the daily phone call?
- Over the phone, do you only discuss surface issues?
- Are you comfortable discussing deeper issues on the phone?

Emotions!

- Do you communicate feelings well over the phone?
- Do you feel emotionally satisfied after the phone call?
- How often do the children get to speak with your partner?

Coming home:

- Do you discuss how you feel about the visits home?
- Do you find your role confusing while your partner is home?
- Are the children confused about what role the parents have while your partner is home for a visit?
- How does re-entry affect you emotionally?
- How does re-entry affect your partner emotionally?
- Who do the children have to confide in about their feelings?
- Are the children comfortable discussing their feelings with your partner?
- How comfortable are you as a couple in re-establishing your sexual relationship upon your partner's return?
- When your partner returns, do you make and effort, or think they should be the one to do all the adjusting?
- Do you talk to your partner about things you find difficult?

Home alone:

- How do you deal with stress when at home alone?
- Do you feel angry/sad/resentful a lot of the time?
- Are you able to talk about these feelings? If so who do you talk to?
- Are you open minded?
- How receptive are you to criticism?
- What do you find most difficult coping with in your partner's absence?
- What coping strategies do you use to help you cope?
- Do you like having all of the responsibility?

CHAPTER THREE
Education and Schools

Introduction:

Should we pay for private education or keep with the government system? Which school would best suit our children? Aren't these typical questions asked by any concerned and interested parent? The difference is, as the 'stay-at-home' partner, the responsibility and final decision is yours.

This chapter has been my stumbling block, the hardest and most emotional to write. Why should I be any different to thousands of other 'stay-at-home' partners, coping alone whilst their partners are working away? Surely choosing a school is one of the normal responsibilities? Something you just get on with? What was the reason for my anger and anxiety? The school I had chosen, after much consideration, proved totally un-supporting when James, then aged fifteen and studying for major exams, began struggling academically. Obviously concerned and anxious to discover the cause of his struggle, I was persistent in my pursuit of answers. It was only after many meetings with the school and constant agitation on my part, that an appointment for James to see an educational psychologist was suggested. This would hopefully determine the reason for his struggle. The educational psychologist's report concluded that James was dyslexic, and recommended some useful strategies which would help alleviate some of his struggle. Disappointingly, the school neatly distanced themselves, more focused on academic achievements than being proactive and supporting James with a plan of action, extra tuition and practical coping strategies. The resulting scenario was a discouraged student lacking in confidence and a concerned, confused parent.

Though dismayed and frustrated by the school's inattention, it strengthened my resolve and motivated me to act independently. Creating a plan of action, I sourced a well experienced tutor who would not only help James with his exam preparation but also help re-build his confidence.

My personal feelings on this subject were so strong, and its effects wide-ranging. I felt it important to document it at the beginning of the chapter. Whilst it was a difficult time, impacting on the family, individually and collectively, it was also enlightening. It made me more aware of the vulnerabilities of the 'stay-at-home' parent and the realisation that if I was to continue this role effectively, I needed to toughen up a little.

Having lived overseas my experience of education is slightly eclectic, encompassing both international schools overseas and the private independent education system within the UK. Hopefully some of this information in the following pages will be helpful and informative, wherever your children are being educated.

Researching schools:

There are many tried and tested methods for researching schools. For general background information, using the internet is an excellent approach, allowing you to be specific and focused in your individual requirements. If possible, it is also a good idea to talk to parents with children already attending the school of your choice.

A strategy we found worked well for us, when researching 6th Form opportunities for James in a new school, was to list specific requirements we, as parents were looking for. James did the same exercise as, of course, his list of qualities was from his own personal perspective. This exercise had a dual purpose. It ensured when visiting prospective schools we were more purposeful and prepared, not overwhelmed by all that we had heard and seen. We were able to achieve a more holistic perspective. By comparing and contrasting our respective notes, we were able to actively discuss and make a final choice, which was satisfactory to everyone.

The checklist when you need to research a school for your child might include the following questions:

- Were the staff intuitive and interested?
- Was there a welcoming, happy atmosphere?
- Was there a sense of community?
- Was a child's holistic development welcomed, not just academic?
- What level of learning support was available?
- Was their curriculum varied?
- Were different levels of sporting ability catered for?
- Were the facilities (specific to your child's requirement, e.g. music, art) of a good level?
- Were cultural and school trips encouraged?
- Was community work encouraged?
- What is the school's policy on bullying, pastoral care?
- Were the students happy and motivated?
- Did the staff project themselves as motivated and caring?
- Was there evidence that staff were encouraged and involved in the extra curricular activities of the school?
- What extra curricular activities did the school promote, Duke of Edinburgh awards, etc

This pre-planning paid dividends. Having been actively encouraged to offer his personal input regarding the final choice of school for his 6th form career, James felt confident and excited, quickly settling into his new routine of weekly boarding. He thrived in his new environment, growing in stature both academically and socially. This was a far cry from two years previously, when he was unhappy at school and struggling academically. His unhappiness and frustration had filtered through to home life, making things at times quite difficult.

I hope this is a useful illustration of how important the pre-planning stage is. The negative knock- on effects of a child who is unhappy and unfulfilled at school will wreak havoc on home life.

Take the time to establish good lines of communication with the school:

Make it your top priority to take the time to acquaint yourself with as many of the children's teachers in the first half term as you possibly can, either by meeting them personally or listening to your children's account of their day. Not only will it help the child with the settling in process, you too will also find it greatly speeds up your own familiarisation with the new school. It is also wise to set up a simple filing system which incorporates all school correspondence. You cannot remember everything and it will be a great help in keeping your finger on the pulse. You will need to hold information on school fees, for example, school trips and any other activities you or the children become involved in. In addition, it will be a gentle discipline, avoiding panics, to ensure you keep documents or letters which provide a feedback for you or a reminder if your queries aren't promptly answered.

The special role of the 'stay-at-home' parent brings extra responsibilities. I have always believed that in order to ensure continuity and progress, school should be a dual responsibility that is shared between home and school. This sharing role is especially beneficial to the 'stay-at-home' partner, as you may find that you are more reliant on the school's understanding and advice in your partner's absence than would otherwise be the case.

Establishing good lines of communication between home and school undoubtedly calls for extra parental input and effort. Whether you opt for volunteering for school trips, fundraising, or sitting on the Board of Governors, these are all activities which will ensure that you meet regularly with people who matter - whether staff or parents. As they take place outside the classroom, in a less formal environment, this involvement always proves an interesting and valuable experience and gives you the opportunity to meet other parents and teachers on a more relaxed and open footing. It will also help you gain a better insight into the daily life and curriculum of the school.

Keep the school informed of personal circumstances:

The stiff upper lip is no longer in fashion and it is perfectly acceptable to keep the school informed of any change in your personal circumstances, if you think it has adversely affected your child. A brief note to the class teacher/personal tutor serves a very constructive purpose and will help remedy the situation. Your child might be experiencing difficulties within the class, for example, which can be attributed to his father's absence. Having been made aware of this fact, the teacher has the opportunity to handle the situation more sensitively.

When Andrew was on his first short term assignment in Yemen, volunteering for the Parent Teacher Association proved a saving grace for me. It helped me get things into perspective, focusing my mind on other things, rather than continually dwelling on his safety and the potential dangers his job might involve. It was really good to be pro-active and involved and, to my surprise, I met many other women in similar circumstances.

Some useful tips:

- Volunteer to help fundraising/school trips, get to know teachers and other parents better, good social outlet.
- Support games matches, fundraising activities, school plays, it helps you become more involved in the school community.

Deal with difficulties quickly:

Be proactive and don't put off difficult issues. Request an appointment to see relevant personnel with whom you can discuss the problem which is worrying you.

I always found it best to deal with things as they happened, whether schoolwork or social issues. Do some research first to make sure you have your facts straight and get any necessary background information you could need to support your case before requesting an appointment with appropriate staff. Within the secondary system a class tutor often replaces the role of a class teacher. This is especially important from your child's perspective, because with one parent away they often need extra reassurance and support. If the issue is dealt with immediately and sensitively by school and parent, it transmits an aura of confidence and encouragement to the child.

If there are specific issues, such as bullying, or your child is having academic problems, make the school aware of the difficulty and ask for an appointment with the appropriate personnel to discuss further. Often if these things are nipped in the bud, the whole thing passes over. Avoid the trap of thinking that if you ignore these hitches they will in time disappear. In my experience quite the opposite occurs. The problem is most unlikely to go away, rather it can equate with the 'rolling stone syndrome' in that the more time passes, the bigger and more emotionally charged the difficulty becomes and inevitably the more negative and tiring the consequences .

Until we repatriated our experience of the British education system had been limited to the relaxed family atmosphere of international schools. Parental participation in school life was actively welcomed and encouraged at the international schools our children attended. I always enjoyed contributing either by being a member of the Parent Teacher Association, fundraising or volunteering for school trips, believing that the school/student/parent relationship is a three-way process, and can only be balanced and successful if each party contributed and participated equally in the association.

Five years ago when we repatriated to UK this naïve belief was challenged and I had a rude awakening! James made a casual remark on his return from school one weekend, saying that he couldn't find his school bag containing all his exam coursework. Several searches of the school grounds did not unearth the bag, but set my parental alarm bells ringing. Maybe it had been stolen? Angered by the unnecessary anguish this incident had caused James and bemused by the house-parent's indifferent attitude to the situation, implying that I was a slightly neurotic mother getting things out of perspective, only strengthened my resolve. Dressing in my best business suit I went into school, requesting an explanation. I was appalled by the school's disinterest and quickly realised that unless I was steadfast in my approach, the situation would not be resolved satisfactorily. I angrily banged the table, demanding to know what action they intended to take in recovering the stolen items. Amazingly, it was only then that I was taken seriously!

This persistence resulted in the safe return of James' bag and coursework and also the disciplining of the offenders. Although this was a thorny situation, it was also enlightening, clearly illustrating as it did the need to be direct and decisive when facing difficult situations. Although deep down you are vulnerable and quaking in your shoes! It reiterated for me that as the 'stay-at-home' parent your continual support, reassurance and belief in your children is necessary and imperative. Especially as those difficult situations always seem to occur once your partner has already left for his/her next assignment. If you are not happy with the school's explanation, follow it up.

Complaints Procedure:

Every school has a set complaints procedure and you can request the guidelines which should be followed. Admittedly, the complexity of the whole education experience can sometimes be intimidating for parents, so it is good to be well prepared. As the lone parent it is even more important to be persistent, when dealing with school issues, either social or academic. If unresolved a minor issue can quickly materialise into something insurmountable, the effects impacting and ricocheting into all areas of family life.

Become conversant with the homework/coursework schedule:

It is wise to do some background reading relating to the child's curriculum. In my personal experience these seem to change surprisingly frequently, even annually, often altering expectations. A lot of GCSE subjects, for instance, incorporate course work with exams. If you have acquired a basic knowledge of the curriculum's expectations of your child, this too will help immensely with the settling in process. You will be relieved to know that there are many informative guides available in bookshops and you can find useful websites on the internet. If you do not understand any particular aspect of the curriculum, then make an appointment to talk it through with the school/relevant teacher.

You can also help by encouraging your child to be well prepared and organised. This saves the dreaded last minute panics. Let your children know that you are always available as a sounding board for homework related matters. By discussing any doubts or problems with a trusted adult, it often throws a different perspective on the whole question.
As the children get older and the curriculum becomes more difficult, it can also be more complex for parents to give objective advice. Then you should encourage them to undertake other means of research, either in a library or on the internet. It is also useful to obtain a list of potential subject tutors (for older children) from the school office, if it transpires that extra help is needed prior to major exams.

Diarise school meetings:

Diarise parent/teacher interviews well in advance and give them top priority, as this may be the only time within the academic calendar that you can check on your child's progress. At parent/teacher evenings I take a few notes, which not only helps keep Dad updated, but also serves as a reference for future meetings. Monitor their progress via these meetings and their annual reports. If it transpires that the children are struggling don't delay taking some action, such as exploring (with the school's help) ways for coping, extra tuition etc.

Pre-plan partner's trips home to coincide with school function:

Often schools produce their academic diary several terms in advance and I have always found it really useful to diarise these dates and functions, forwarding them onto Andrew in good time. This advance information enables him to then plan accordingly and attend several school functions per year. It helped him to also keep a finger on the academic pulse and the children enjoyed being able to share their achievements and progress with both of us.

Emergency contacts:

Provide the school with an emergency contact name and number. Ensure it is someone dependable and practical

In the event of emergency or sickness all schools require a contact name and number. A useful exercise is to identify someone (friend or family) before the child starts at the school, who is well-known both to parent and child. Then you are reassured that the potential contact is happy and available to act in 'loco parentis'.

If your child is at boarding school and you live overseas you will be requested by the school to provide the details of the child's legally appointed guardian, who acts on your behalf in your absence. Some duties of an appointed Guardian can involve attending parent/teacher interviews or even working with the school on issues of discipline/bullying if it arises. Looking after the student for Exeat and half term holidays, overseeing travel arrangements to the airport from school and responsibility for medical issues in absence of parent are all duties which fall within the Guardian's remit.

Pre-exam anxieties?

When dealing with children's anxieties during the pre-exam period, it is very easy to feel as if you are becoming overwhelmed by the pressure. I found the following useful when dealing with teenagers and exams pressure:

- During exams and revision time, things can be very tense at home, especially when you are alone and have no-one to share with. The best plan to do is make life as easy as possible and arrange easy meals, for instance, for the period of exams.

- Encourage your child to continue normal sports and activities during the exam period. It helps them to take a break from revision, get some exercise and social interaction.

- Request the exam timetable well in advance of exams and be well briefed on what subjects are being taken and on what day. Such basic advance thought ensured that if I knew it was a subject they found especially difficult I could react and be available to support them accordingly.

- If the atmosphere at home gets a bit intense, it can quickly lead to a confrontation with the child. One well tried coping strategy I quickly learnt was to put some distance between myself and the house. Either going out for a long walk, a workout in the gym, digging up the garden or taking lots of bottles to the recycling centre all proved very therapeutic.

- If you are not careful, well-meant parental support can unintentionally turn into parental invasion, causing resentment. By all means make general enquiries about exams. If the teen wants to talk about things worrying them, let them know that you can always make time to talk it over. If not, do not pursue it, they are already feeling under great pressure and may view Mum's interest, however well intentioned, as superfluous to requirements.

- A personal tutor is an excellent benefit during this fraught time. There is a great advantage to employing an outside force, apart from being more tuned into the current methods of revision/study. As is well documented, a teenager will more willingly take advice from someone outside the family, rather than a parent! This despite the fact that the information imparted is often a duplicate of what you have been saying. Coming from a new and different perspective, it will generally have more impact. We found this really worked for both of us during James's exams several years ago. Added to which it enabled me to share the load, with James able to contact the tutor between sessions if he needed to.

- When on your own it is easy to over pressurise children on the school and study front. Make sure you regularly arrange outings, trips to the cinema, shopping or a weekend visiting friends. It is amazing how these little treats can change the dynamics, quickly re-establishing a status quo.

- If possible arrange a fun weekend away, it takes the stress off everyone for a while.

- If your child is happy, confident and challenged at school it will make the whole 'stay-at-home' alone experience more positive. However, wise parents will openly acknowledge that children who go through their school career without experiencing minor obstacles are in the minority. If you can take some simple steps to be well prepared for these eventualities and have proven strategies to help you cope, it will be a lot less traumatic.

- As the 'stay-at-home' partner, demands on you are already great. If a child is not happy at school it can have devastating repercussions on the balance and health of the whole family. Get proactive and look at areas of stress and find ways to reduce it. Flexibility is the keyword to success.

International Schools:

Some families are on an overseas posting when the assignee is re-assigned to a short term project in a different country. International schools are often the hub of the expatriate community and will provide a valuable cushion of emotional, academic and social support for you and your family in your partner's absence. Of necessity, International Schools are far more flexible with their entrance requirements, responding to the transitory lifestyle of the international communities they serve. If you are currently on a posting overseas and there is the possibility of returning to your home country within the next 12 months, whether for reasons of continuity of education/dual career, a good rule of thumb is to plan your research about 12 months in advance. Do not assume that the long summer holiday will be time enough to get all sorted. Allowing ample time for the whole research and transition process will ensure that all your questions have been answered as well as leaving time for any last minute hitches.

Many International Schools operate a mentor system for new parents which helps you to initiate email correspondence with parents already in posting, who can offer you experience of both the school and the destination country. This will help build up your bigger picture and in turn enable your children to be more prepared for the new school/culture. Taking advantage of such support helps to highlight issues which may be problematic and dispel many of your worries. Such contact and information will also be an excellent basis on which to make better informed and more grounded decisions, having researched the pros and cons first and arrived at a more rounded and satisfactory conclusion.

Private independent schools within the UK:

Entrance to most private schools in the UK is dependant on the child passing an entrance exam. Traditionally these entrance exams are sat in the winter term and most private schools offer several bursaries annually. Popular subject areas for bursaries are the Sciences, Music and Sport. Parents will need to research these opportunities, as individual schools differ. Be warned, though, competition is high for these prizes. Generally scholarship exams are also taken during the winter term for the following autumn intake.

The house system:

Students are divided into different Houses within the school. Each House is allocated a Head and a Deputy Head from amongst the school staff and they will organise House meetings often on a weekly basis. These meetings address a wide variety of subjects, ranging from the academic to drugs and bullying. The role of House staff is to provide students with a contact point for communication and pastoral care, as well as supporting and monitoring their academic progress.

If there are unresolved issues, which have not been dealt with to your satisfaction at teacher level, the general rule is that the next stage is to request a meeting with the Head of the School. If at that level you still have not received complete satisfaction, the school will recommend that you formally lodge your concern in writing to the Board of Governors, where it will be debated and concluded at their monthly meeting. The majority of this information is provided by the school as an information booklet prior to the student's entrance. It may also be available on the school website.

State schools within the UK:

- Research the school and its OFSTED reports, look on websites, talk to parents locally.
- Visit a variety of schools to gain an overall perspective of what is available.
- State schools often offer more accountability, there are more avenues of recourse for parents to follow. If there is a query, the first point of contact is the Tutor, second point of contact is the Head, third contact is the Board of Governors, ultimately ending with the Local Education Authority.
- Look for good primary and secondary schools in your catchment area.
- Larger schools often have more finances, therefore better resources, computer labs, language labs, sports facilities, and more provision for special needs education.
- Does the school have canteen facilities, where do the children eat school meals?
- If the children go to a local school, they quickly become part of the local community, building up contacts and friends.
- Does the school offer good after-school clubs, breakfast clubs? Is there a school nurse?
- Important to regularly attend school functions, parent's evening and put faces to names of teachers. This is especially important as the children progress through their secondary education, where subjects are taught by individual teachers.
- Important to establish good communication with the parents of your child's friends. This will in time become a good support network.
- Smaller schools are not necessarily better. Smaller rural schools may combine a number of years in one and the same classroom.
- State schools often offer a wider variety of subjects for GCSE and A level, due to the larger pupil ratio

Family feedback:

Our experiences in dealing with the children's education have been diverse, interesting and at times emotional.

Andrew said: 'When a problem occurs, I feel guilty that I am not there to lend support. Emotionally, it all falls on your partner's shoulders. This impacted on our family when just before major exams, James was diagnosed as dyslexic and the school offered no support. Fortunately Marian responds well in emergency situations. She quickly did some research and sourced a tutor who could help James with revision skills and strategies. The tutor's support was invaluable, it not only gave James confidence academically, but also gave us feedback. Once this support network was in place, it was a huge relief to everyone.'

Marian said: 'It is so important to have good communication with the school. If the school and parent are pro-active in their mutual roles, it ensures that difficult issues are immediately dealt with. Feedback is forthcoming, creating a healthy, intuitive relationship, rather than a confrontational one. I hated doing parent's evenings alone, manically trying to gather all the information I was being fed about progress and problems, ever aware that it had to then be fed back to Andrew. Seeing other parents attending these functions with partners echoed my loneliness and the responsibility of my solo-role.'

James, then aged sixteen said: 'Since changing schools I am much happier, really enjoying school and more focused academically.'

Laura said: 'It was sometimes hard when Dad wasn't around for parent's evenings and school functions. When you saw your friends at these functions with both their parents there it really impacted how much Dad missed by being away.'

QUICK TIPS

- Establish good communication with the school
- Get involved with school life, PTA fundraising, volunteering for school trips
- Monitor the child's academic progress by regularly attending parent teacher interviews
- Ensure the assignee is able to attend several school functions per year
- If you are worried about your child talk to the school
- Get to know the staff and individual teachers
- Keep the school updated of your personal circumstances
- Research curriculum expectations
- Does the school have a good complaints procedure?
- Does the school have a good anti bullying policy?
- If your child is struggling talk to the school, discuss the possibility of extra tutoring.

CHAPTER FOUR
Family Responsibilities

Introduction:

When I was re-reading this chapter prior to its final editing, I experienced a horrid sinking feeling when I realised there was some overlap with topics I have covered previously in Chapters 1 and 2. I was torn. Should I be mercenary and omit the whole chapter? Or was it better to make amendments to the text, merely shortening the chapter?

My personal feelings were that 'family responsibilities', such an important and integral part of the of 'stay-at-home' scenario, required a strong presence within the book. In conclusion I decided the latter course of action was best. Amending the text, has shortened the chapter and my apologises for any repetition, but I am hopeful that this will not detract from the important message this chapter conveys.

Be flexible and intuitive:

Simple re-thinking and re-adjusting will produce new solutions.

It is worth bearing in mind that often children feel more vulnerable with one parent away. If you are able from the outset to acknowledge the difficulties they are encountering, put aside judgements and create the right environment where they will feel comfortable to chat, this will reap many benefits. With time and perseverance, youngsters will begin to value these opportunities to chat together. By providing them with their own personal space, you will be surprised at the range of subjects opening up to discussion and ultimately get to know your children in a different light.

My own personal experience of trying to be 'both mum and dad' to two teenagers often strained my emotional resources. Whilst I understood the importance of 'being there', dispensing understanding, support, motivation and intuition, to name but a few needs, I did sometimes resent the fact that I was continually doing it alone. Being in this situation, you are always both the 'fall guy' and disciplinarian, an incredibly difficult combination of roles and a bitter pill to swallow. Being Mum, the intuitive tendency is to become emotionally involved, you are always a participant, desperately needing to become more of an onlooker! In my experience, the one thing I did find was I became over protective and too involved. Life with teenagers is never dull, and inevitably there were sometimes difficulties with school and friends. Instead of sitting back and letting things evolve naturally, I was the 'coper and fixer' and my instinctive reaction was to interfere, trying to sort things out for them. My teenagers naturally resented this interference and told me so. Being the 'stay-at-home' parent is a double-edged sword, because you are often coping alone with the daily responsibilities of home and family. You find yourself becoming more intuitive though, your coping strategy being that you are more emotionally wired into your family's needs and moods. Although my experience has been with teenagers, it will to a greater or lesser extent apply to children of all ages. A word of caution here: thinking they can't cope without your involvement is a misnomer. Learning to quietly take a step back and listen is hard but worthwhile. It doesn't mean you care any less, you are giving them the space and responsibility to develop as individuals.

On a positive note, however, the experience has literally re-educated us. We are more aware and sensitive to the fact that as individuals within the family, we encounter and cope differently with the challenges of this lifestyle. As a family we are now more able, through listening and talking together, to value each other's experiences.

Knowing that we are able to talk things through, recognise and give each other space, encouragement, empathy and motivation, has helped strengthen the bond. Our teenagers' constant questions and interest in the progress of this book during the last two years has undoubtedly been one of my motivating forces for its completion and publication, for instance. And that is a real bonus.

Review your priorities regularly:

Get out and do something different and enjoyable for yourself. Just because you are 100% responsible, does not mean that you have to dedicate yourself to the family 24/7. Coping alone with the ups-and-downs of family life can leave you feeling mentally drained and physically exhausted. A well-chosen change of activity outside your home will soon fire you up and leave you feeling refreshed and ready to return in a coping frame of mind.

Time to pursue an interest of your own is of equal importance to the youngsters having hobbies. It might mean joining a writing club or going to the gym. Because you are to a great extent alone dealing with the highs and lows of family life, it is all too easy to become single-minded and allow rigidity to set in, making huge efforts to get everything done to the very last detail – and to perfection. Flexibility soon flies out of the window and you are caught on a never-ending treadmill. I found the best way to deal with this dangerous situation was to review my priorities and remember that as circumstances change so should your priorities.

If your work and life are getting too pressurised, sit down and quietly assess the current setup. Look at how you can arrange your schedule around the family's requirements, so that there is a better balance between the two. In the early days of our initiation into short-term assignments, I was too intense, mistakenly thinking the only way I would successfully keep everything balanced in Andrew's absence was for the children's routine to fill the gap. We struggled with this unnatural existence for several weeks, but soon realised that I needed, for all of our sakes, to find a healthier alternative to this insular existence. Listing interests I had always wanted to pursue further was my starting point. I was mercenary, rigorously eliminating the majority of suggestions. This left me with two choices:

    a) do a refresher course in French conversation and
    b) participate in several writing workshops in London.

Creating this new focus was the key and within two weeks I had signed up for a 6 month refresher French class at our local University and also booked and paid for two writing workshops. Suddenly life wasn't so difficult and intense, because I was getting out, meeting different people and had a more interesting agenda. I was soon feeling much more relaxed. On the home front things became more manageable, more holistic and less child-orientated.

So if you find yourself on the precipice, considering taking that job, doing that college course etc, don't feel guilty. By taking the plunge, your time may be more limited, but you will definitely benefit from the outside influences you yourself have generated. You will meet new people and have new experiences, making you a more interesting person when you do spend time together with your family.

The sandwich generation:

The scope of your family responsibilities may also include caring for elderly parents. Known as the 'sandwich generation', you are squeezed between responsibilities for both adolescent offspring and your parents. This brings extra challenges to the already overflowing portfolio of the 'stay-at-home' partner. If you have siblings living nearby, agree a timetable and share some of the practical responsibilities of shopping, healthcare and housework involved in caring for your elderly parents. Even if you don't have the convenience of family members living near by, by keeping them up-to-date regularly it will support you and help you offload some of the emotional responsibilities. Rather than soldiering on in isolation, you have to become good at delegating.

Regularly reacquaint yourself with your children:

This may sound rather surprising and obvious, but be aware of the need to acquaint – and perhaps re-acquaint yourself with the age and stage at which your children find themselves. This is especially helpful and important in the absence of family and close friends. When the kids hit their teenage years Andrew was already working away and I found it very useful to do some background reading on teenage issues, as well as attending talks organised by the school on drugs, alcohol and relationship issues for teens.

These talks were a useful way of introducing me to the mainstream UK thinking on adolescent issues. Having previously lived within the environs of a small, somewhat protected expatriate society for ten years, I realised how out of touch I was. I discovered that there were many issues, so much a part of the fabric of daily life here in the UK, which as a family we had never previously experienced. I had lots to catch up on and needed to learn quickly! These talks were also useful from a social viewpoint, as they provided a venue where you networked with other parents; a reminder that other people had the same problems and that you weren't on your own.

All the normal parental routines, attending parent/teacher interviews, school plays etc, which you have been used to sharing can, with time, become quite onerous and isolating. You have to be practical and get on with it despite the fact that attending school functions in particular used to make me feel very vulnerable and aware of my single-parent status. At times I even caught myself feeling quite envious of other parents in their couples, supporting each other and enjoying the experience.

Kids and their social lives:

Another coping strategy is to encourage regular meetings with friends, whether organising a sleep-over, cinema outings or sports fixtures. If you have older children it is a good plan to encourage their sociability and independence. The difficulty in allowing your children more independence is how much do you compromise? A good rule of thumb, which helps you stay safely on the parental guidelines, is to identify several boundaries which you have previously agreed with your teenager: safety considerations, time due in etc. Whether their venue is a music concert or a party at a friend's house, allow them the independence of maybe travelling one way by public transport, whilst you meet them at the end of the evening. Not only does this encourage independence but the companionship of friends will help detract from Mum or Dad's absence.

Never overlook the importance of introducing other people into your children's daily routine, whether it is a sports coach, their grandparents or youth group leader. Encouraging these hobbies became an integral part of our family framework.

These extra-curricular activities ensured they had a responsibility to attend respective classes and take regular exercise, whilst creating new opportunities to meet and socialise with other youngsters sharing similar interests. Above all it gave focus and structure to their free time and ensured they benefited from the excellent role model their respective teachers/coaches provided.

Encourage independence:

If your children are teenagers encourage them to become more independent by getting a holiday job, taking public transport etc. It is really worthwhile encouraging teens in the independence drive. Start gradually by making them responsible for making and attending doctor's appointments, This is a good ploy, not only does it give them space to discuss things in privacy, it provides them with another conduit within which they can discuss both physical and emotional issues which might be worrying them. Encourage them to get a weekend job to give them an idea of the working world and managing their own money; offer them driving lessons; give them a monthly clothing allowance.

For the 'stay-at-home' partner well used to being organised and totally responsible for the running of home and family's welfare, actively encouraging a surly teenager to take some responsibility is definitely challenging, but worth persevering with - believe me!

Ground rules:

It took me time to realise a key fact: what may have worked when there were two parents on the scene full-time, could not realistically be upheld when you were on your own. I learnt with time that the whole family relationship benefited if we regularly re-evaluated the situation and prioritised several sensible ground rules that everyone was familiar with. Not only did this give us a framework to work within, it also ensured that in not monitoring every movement we were more relaxed etc. By insisting on sharing household chores, for instance, children soon realise that to have a good and happy home life everyone has to work as a team. Your own job is made a bit easier and it helps make children more independent, ultimately giving more free time at the end of the day to do things as a family etc.

Resentment:

It is important to remember that whatever age your children, there is a likelihood that you will encounter some form of resentment because Mum or Dad is away. Often this resentment will be aimed at you, and it will not always be obvious, manifesting itself in a variety of ways and behaviours.

I strongly advise you to do a bit of background reading on the stage of your children, not only does it serve as gentle preparation for potential pitfalls, but also makes you more understanding and therefore able to cope better (hopefully) when these nuances do occur. Whilst you should exercise your own judgment and try not to make too much of these issues, it is good to be aware and be prepared. It is sensible to realize that one cannot always operate on intuition alone when dealing with a stroppy toddler or a rebelling, hormonal adolescent!

Get rid of the guilt:

You are only human so don't beat yourself up when things go wrong. Maybe you can't help with their physics homework, but pinpoint areas in which you can help (languages, literature). Be realistic, offer help/support when possible, provide suggestions for areas you are unable to help them in, offering alternative suggestions such as the library or the web.

Family quality time:

Working at establishing good quality time is vital. Not only does it break the weeks up when your partner is away, but it also gets you out of the house, away from normal routine and into the fresh air. By giving each individual in the family unit the opportunity to do something regularly which is of specific interest to them, (bowling, cinema, canoeing, swimming, shopping, museum) it gives everyone something to look forward to. Inviting family members to choose one activity keeps the involvement and sense of continuity of family life. Try and meet up with friends or family to all do the chosen activity together. From personal experience Sundays are the worst day and it is amazing how, with a bit of forethought and by organising something different to do, it changes the overall family atmosphere and, consequently, the day.

One 'stay-at-home' Mum of six children and long experienced in this lifestyle was happy to share some of her own tried and tested coping strategies: 'With a large family and husband often away for several months at a time, timetables play a large part in our lives. By planning in advance, I endeavour to allocate each of my children individual time on a regular monthly basis. I tailor these outings to the individual's age and interests.

Whether a walk in the park or a trip to the cinema, knowing they had that 'special time' to look forward to was very important, giving them privacy and the opportunity to talk things through on a one-to-one basis. If they had worries, we used this time to help get things into perspective. These times were hugely beneficial both to the children and myself as I was able to enjoy the children as individuals. It was an unobtrusive way to keep the finger on the family pulse'.

Find a friend!

Coping alone is a solitary pastime and coping alone with children can be doubly difficult. With this lifestyle, the age and stage of your children is a first consideration. Generally, if you have Junior School age children or younger, barriers for both mother and child are quickly broken down. The regularity of meeting other parents at the school gate is a useful contact point, or with pre-school children you inevitably make friends through nursery or playgroups. However, if your children are at secondary level as mine were, it becomes more difficult. You are merely a facilitator, transporting them from A to B and rarely making any contact with other parents. The natural tendency for many partners coping on their own is to shoulder the entire load responsibilities. This may be sustainable for a short time, but long term it is unhealthy. Chum up with someone locally or join a gym where you will meet others regularly and make friends.

My friend Tina's welcoming kitchen was my port in a storm. Through the years her large scrubbed pine kitchen table proved a comforting forum for sharing, counseling, laughing and occasional tears, as we navigated the peaks and troughs of our family's lives.

Create extra time and space :

One good way to create extra time in which to enjoy some personal space is to get up an hour before everyone else. This book is indeed a testament to this strategy. By trying this out I found myself at my most creative and productive pre-dawn and pre-interruptions. Much of this book was written in the early hours of the morning!

Make a point of putting time aside to talk about big issues as a family when your partner is home. The topics could range from the choice of subjects for exams, getting a pet or discussing the next holiday location. One tactic which really worked for us was to agree in advance to set aside an evening, to discuss the important issues likely to arise in the near future.

Having been kept up-to-date regularly via emails and phone calls anyway, we could rationally address matters without wasting time going over the whole history of the situation and often at the end of an evening have also come up with a solution. This method gave us a common forum, where things had been agreed jointly. Consequently, should an issue come up whilst Andrew was away, we could easily refer back and not get entrenched in the whys and wherefores, kid's reports, behaviour etc. Everyone was accountable and knew it.

Get cooking:

No matter what their age, encourage the children to start cooking and help in the kitchen. You may need to rely on them in an emergency and it is also a good precursor to surviving at university/college.

Be prepared:

Have a dependable local point of contact, on which either you or the children can call on in an emergency. Have an agreed procedure which everyone is familiar with and keep the contact details readily available on a kitchen board. You never know when you might need it.

Feedback from the kids:

Jo Parfitt's two boys, Sam and Josh, kindly proffered their thoughts whilst Mum provided me with some background: 'For seven years our family life was based on a father who has commuted weekly and lived in a Bed and Breakfast most of this time when working away. He certainly had not made a home elsewhere, so when he came home he had the week's family administration to catch up on, as well as his own work administration, being freelance. We tended to only have quality time when we were on holiday'.

Sam then aged thirteen said: 'I'm glad he earns a good wage, so I can see why he does it. Also many friends at school are in the same situation. Of course I go to a good school, so I suppose that's why. But it would be better to have some time together at the weekend, when he's not doing work. I wish he didn't bring work home. We don't get much time together when he is home either. I don't notice it too much. I guess I find it OK. But I like him to be around, even if we don't have to go out anywhere'.

Josh, then aged twelve said: 'It's weird because when I go to a friend's house and their Dad is there it makes me feel funny because when they come to my house, it's just my Mum. And if my Dad is there he's always upstairs doing work. I wish Dad was here so he could help me with my homework and we could do more stuff together. .

Laura then fourteen years old commented: 'I miss Dad not coming to sports days and parents evening at school. Because he is not here he doesn't get involved in the school part of my life. I miss being able to do things as a family at weekends. Because she had to be organised Mum could sometimes be quite rigid, she is not as laid back as Dad. Sometimes that was hard. In the long run though, it did make me more independent.'

From the perspective of a younger child, six year old Anne - whose father has been doing short term assignments for the last 2 years - says: 'I get miserable when I think about Daddy, so I try not to think about him at all.'

James, then sixteen years old, likened his Dad's absences to a bereavement: 'When Dad returns overseas, it is like we are in mourning for a short time, before we get back to 'normal'. I am used to it now, the hardest thing I find is not being able to be spontaneous, everything has to be arranged. Sometimes it feels that there is too much for just Mum to cope with. It seems that she is compensating for Dad not being here and sometimes tries too hard. This lifestyle is very practical and pigeonholed, sometimes I wish it could be more spontaneous.'

QUICK TIPS

- Talk regularly as a family
- Regularly review your priorities
- Learn to share family responsibilities with others in your extended family
- Regularly re-acquaint yourself with your children
- It is important for children to develop hobbies and a good social life
- Encourage children to be independent
- Expect feelings of resentment - it is natural
- Get rid of the guilt
- Make space for family quality time
- Find a friend
- Make extra time and space
- Get cooking
- Plan for possible emergency situations
- Encourage family feedback

CHAPTER FIVE
Finances and Budgeting

Pre-planning:

Pre-planning seems to be the buzzword best applied to all short term assignment issues raised so far in this book and I can vouch for the importance of this. Being as well prepared as possible and, in order to achieve this, setting yourself tangible pre-planning objectives is a prerequisite for the 'stay-at-home' partner who wants to maintain the status quo on the home front! As we well know, whether your partner's posting is in Beijing or Brighton, unforeseen expenses and emergencies have a canny way of making their presence felt, just when you think you are sailing along comfortably.

Being prepared will not only help your peace of mind, it will also reduce the necessity for many expensive phone calls.

If, like me, you had been on an expatriate posting for some years, financial responsibilities were out of sight and intangible. Responsibilities such as mortgages were surreal and something I knew very little about in any detail.

The only reminder of these serious financial commitments was the occasional figures on a bank statement. Until repatriation hit, that is, when suddenly I was put in a position where I too had to understand the implications in depth and inevitably had to handle any problems arising.

Doing your homework:

So if you want to avoid this steep learning curve, which will inevitably be necessary at the least convenient moment, it is an extremely worthwhile exercise to spend a bit of time doing some accounting homework. A useful first step would be to break down your expenses into separate monthly and annual amounts, so that you have an oversight of what you will have to budget for. Then try and forecast likely larger expenses covering items such as unexpected car repairs and annual holidays, not forgetting to also allow a 'safety-net' sum for emergencies etc. It is worthwhile networking with good friends who are in a similar family situation as yourself, to get a rough idea of what they set aside for car servicing, for instance, if you are not sure what to allow. Although a phone call to your local garage will also be helpful in obtaining approximate costs. An equally important factor for which you should make allowances is the cost of communication. It is an essential contributor to the success and sustainability of the short term assignment lifestyle.

Get organised:

For most of us budgeting and financial responsibilities are a tolerated evil, often brushed under the carpet until the next bill comes in. If you are rigorous and establish pre-planning financial responsibilities as part of your own regular routine, whether annual or monthly in your organisers, you will be able to present any problems needing resolving in a competent manner, or warn in advance of large bills coming up and which have to be allowed for. It will encourage communication between the two of you and the sharing of responsibilities. It also helps to save you a lot of emotional angst in the long run!

Accounting systems:

As I now handle most of the financial responsibilities it has widened my horizon beyond just the household budget, I have seen for myself the absolute necessity for good and regular record keeping. In many ways, using your home computer to help you do this will make it a far easier task. If you need to learn how to use spreadsheets for accounting purposes, there is a wide choice of courses available and also books you can use as ongoing support. I am really proud of my understanding of our overall financial position at any given point in time. It has also clearly brought home to me the need for saving and the necessity for making pension arrangements.

The best way to pay?

In order to get a clearer representation of monthly outgoings, it is useful to establish standing orders or direct debit facilities with the bank. These are very easy to set up through your different suppliers e.g. gas, electricity, telephone. In fact, they actively encourage you to spread your payments over the year and so help manage the considerable variations in consumption, e.g. heating more expensive in the winter. Some even offer a small discount or cashback as an incentive for you to get a direct debit arrangement set up.

These payments are automatically deducted on a monthly basis and you can choose whether you want them all as direct debits to come out of your account, say on the 1st of the month, or whether you prefer to spread them over the whole month, depending on what date you receive a salary and other payments to cover them. This arrangement reduces the need for sending out so many cheques. The suppliers are very efficient these days at regularly sending you the bills, so you are still in control of your overall budget and it is not difficult to keep tabs on how much everything is costing. It is of course very important to monitor your outgoings and if you find the monthly amounts agreed by you with the supplier are too high and you are in credit, a phone call is all that is needed to arrange for them to be reduced to a more realistic level.

These facilities ensure that lengthy accounting is kept to a minimum. However, do not forget annual outgoings such as different insurances, your AA/RAC membership and other subscriptions you may have to pay for such as sports clubs for you and the children. Be aware and budget also for annual subscriptions to the various professional organisations which the short term assignee may have to belong to. Because they are tied up with work they can often be an unknown quantity until they are due for payment. Membership of these professional-related organisations is costly, amounting to hundreds of pounds, or thousands of pounds depending on your partner's industry and area of expertise.

Once these direct debits or standing orders have been set up, it is then a good time to scrutinise your monthly finances. You now have a much clearer overall perspective of monthly outgoings and can also work out what is left to cover other expenses. It can take a bit of effort to make yourself get on top of such tasks, but the reward is an inner strength in the knowledge that you have your finances under control and there should be no awful panics or unexpected demands for money you had not allowed for.

I found a really useful exercise was to look at a few personal finance websites: an especially helpful one is Martin Lewis's money saving website, www.moneysavingexpert.com, which shows you an excellent monthly budget format I now use , as well as good current advice on saving and money saving ideas.

Authorisation:

Ensure before your partner departs that all agreements, such as bank accounts, utility bills and credit cards are in your name/ joint-names and prepare a letter of authorisation from your partner, thus avoiding continually being quoted the merits of the Data Protection Act by operators. This is a frustration which I encountered many times on repatriation and once your partner is away on assignment it can be far more difficult and complex to organise!

- Make sure that your partner writes to these organisations giving his authorisation for you to act on his behalf when necessary.

- In the case of any agreements held in joint names, such as mortgages and credit cards, make sure that you have your partner's written authority to act on their behalf and that you and the company in question have a copy of the authority.

The serious stuff - Wills and Legal issues:

The pre-planning stage is also the time to ensure that you both have current wills. I cannot stress enough the importance of also updating these regularly, not just when your partner embarks on a new overseas assignment, as your circumstances never stand still and you may have to take account of this when thinking of inheritance issues.

Talk of wills and financial responsibilities is a sobering business for many people. However, working overseas in often dangerous and isolated locations it is a necessity. Personally, once these onerous "i's" have been dotted and the "t's" crossed, I felt quite relieved and more relaxed about then concentrating on more pleasurable issues, such as planning the family holiday.

Insurances:

Some useful questions to ask yourself might be:

- What and whom does the company insurance cover?
- Does your partner's insurance cover for death and disability?
- What are the limits of benefits offered?

Keep the records updated, advising the insurer of any change in circumstances or medical situation.

Medical insurance is also another essential consideration for the family budget. Whilst some employers may provide medical insurance for both the employee and family as part of the assignee's 'package', this is not generally the norm, so check beforehand what your responsibilities are and that of the company. A word of warning: even if you do have medical insurance as part of the employee contract, you should check the terms of the insurance very carefully. To cut their costs, some employers have considerably reduced the benefits of the medical insurance offered. And whilst outwardly it can sound reassuring, there can be some surprises lurking, such as the many limitations which the medical insurers themselves impose. Always take time to read the small print.

Several large private medical insurance companies offer special packages tailored to the needs of expatriates. They include AXA, PPP Healthcare and BUPA. Whether you are protected under your company for medical insurance or insuring yourself, it is wise to do some research to obtain the best cover and cost. Do not forget to update your cover for new postings.

Uncertainty:

It is important to budget for those lean times, and some sensible financial advice we received from our financial advisors was to ensure that we always had the equivalent of three month's salary in our emergency fund. Whilst the thought of dipping into the emergency fund was sometimes tempting, knowing the money was available was a good security blanket in times of uncertainty.

Financial Goals:

It is not only sportsmen these days who need to be goal-orientated. A wide proportion of the population, from students to those facing retirement, are affected by this new/popular way of thinking, and the 'stay-at-home' partners are no exception. For them, the goals will most probably be connected with providing your family with a good standard of living and education. You will probably also set your self saving targets and this may also involve some far-reaching investment decisions.

In order to make the goals realistic, however, it is helpful to break them down into manageable units of time, say for instance yearly, six monthly and monthly. Then you set achievable goals for the given periods. Another consideration when establishing financial/budgeting goals is to mutually agree and clarify individual responsibilities.

Perhaps your partner is an avid 'investment-aholic' enjoying the challenge of monitoring the progress and maintenance of family investments and he is able to do this quite easily on the web whilst on assignment. The 'stay-at-home' partner, more traditionally, is responsible for the daily maintenance and budget of the family – she will be operating at more of a micro-level, but her responsibilities are just as important as those of her partner.

How you organise the division of responsibilities between yourselves is a very personal decision, but what this does is to set out individual boundaries, whilst also recognising and maintaining the team effort which is such an important ingredient of the short term assignment lifestyle.

Your yearly goal with regards to budgeting etc, could be to book a holiday, go on a course, or have the garden re-designed. Medium term goals could be to move house, buy a new car or go back to college and re-train in a different profession.

Once you have established your own particular goals, then the next step is to obtain several quotations for carrying out the projects you have identified. Having an informed idea of the cost involved for your plans means that you can then budget accordingly. Getting into the habit of doing this type of research and budgeting, as a natural part of your role, is beneficial from many different points of view. At a personal level, having the financial facts to hand gives you confidence and makes you a much better manager and coper. At the expatriate assignee's level it helps them feel a part of what is going on at home, because you are able to provide all the facts and figures necessary for making decisions and this is a big load you can take off his shoulders.

In addition to this, the nature of short term work can involve the employee moving straight from one posting to another, often without leaving any time to 'ground themselves' at home between assignments. So these different projects can serve as the glue in the relationship, whilst also giving the 'stay-at-home' a focus, to work and report on.

The reality of this type of work is that the 'stay-at-home' partner, often without realising, gets totally immersed in the supporting role on the home front, whilst the employee is totally absorbed by his project/job. This existence is only punctuated by phone calls or emails, until the weekend visit or leave period, making the homecoming potentially quite a stressful time.

If you have agreed yearly/six monthly goals it gives everyone some common ground to focus on and pick up, as it were, where you left off at the last meeting. It also serves to highlight clearly some of the reasons why you are leading this lifestyle as you work towards your mutual reward/objective, be it a new car, holiday or paying the school fees.

Reading the small print – your responsibilities:

A Useful Checklist

- Be aware of your responsibilities regarding your rather complicated tax status and the procedures involved. Contact your local tax office for updated information and consider taking specialist advice.

- National Insurance contributions – if you want to be eligible for a state pension you can pay voluntary contributions whilst overseas. Contact the office at Longbenton for further information: Inland Revenue, Centre for Non-residents, Room BP1301, Benton Park View, Newcastle-on-Tyne.

- Get banking advice from banks who operate globally and are specialists in financial matters of expatriates.

- Research the types of medical insurance available. Read the small print carefully, to find out what are you covered for. Be informed about when they pay for repatriation, evacuation etc. When you change countries and take up a new assignment, a quick phone call to update yourself is advisable.

Financial update:

Update your financial education, re-acquainting yourself with the various aspects of your family's financial portfolio.

- Keep at least an annual check on what investments you have, investment amounts, names of investment portfolios, date of investment and amount invested originally, maturity of investment etc. Keep documentation properly filed.

- Do you and your partner have life assurance? What is the company name covering your life assurance, what amount are you insured for? Have your circumstances changed since the original assurance was initiated? Does the amount need to be increased/decreased? Do you pay the premium on a monthly/yearly basis? What is the premium amount?

- If you have a mortgage, who is it with? What sort of mortgage do you have? What is the monthly outgoing of your mortgage? How much longer does your mortgage run for? What is the current amount owing on your mortgage?

- Wills and inheritance tax. It is essential that wills are kept updated of changing circumstances. During our expatriate career we always ensured we took financial advice from a well established business specialising in expatriate and financial issues.

- Pre-departure, make sure that all agreements, such as bank accounts, utility accounts, credit cards are in your name/joint names and that you, the bank and the utility company have his authorisation for you to act on his behalf when necessary.

Family feedback:

Andrew said: 'As with family matters, you have to be prepared to hand over totally to your partner. When you return the cost of living can be a shock and finances can become a major disagreement. The trick is to prioritise, talk things through regularly and prioritise individual responsibilities. It is important that the 'stay-at-home' partner has understanding of the complexities and responsibilities of the family finances so that she is able to deal with them in your absence.'

Marian said: 'Although I was used to dealing with the finances I didn't like it. My best coping strategies were a well organised accounting system, talking things through with Andrew and saving regularly for the emergency fund.'

THE EPILOGUE

Now the writing of the book is almost complete, I am beginning to get emotional! Whilst the journey has been cathartic, all consuming and often frustrating, it has been also inspiring.

Frankly, I am glad to be achieving some form of closure on this project, it has been an immensely emotional experience, to have lived for the past two years. Attempting to gain a greater insight into the experience has involved placing mine and contributing families, characters and relationships under the microscope. People's generosity of spirit, honesty and willingness to share their experiences has been remarkable. Tinging my mood of relief, I also feel a sense of poignancy and bereavement, 'the book' has been my main motivator during the last year, stretching, provoking and challenging me. Increasing my confidence, it has enabled me to confront different, and difficult issues and situations and has been the catalyst in showing and helping me satisfactorily resolve, at least some of these issues!

In conclusion I ask myself three questions:

Would I have done anything differently?

Most definitely and always wise in hindsight! I would have issued several pre-requisites pre-assignment.

- Necessity to get family feedback, explore and discuss as a family by listing individual family member's potential coping abilities, as well as the positive and negative effects of this lifestyle.

- Do some background reading, talk to people with 'hands on' experience of this lifestyle.

- Take a realistic look at the support network available? Will it support you? How can you improve it?

- Joint agreement of specified period of time this type of assignment can be done for? Review the ongoing situation on a 6 monthly or yearly basis.

Would I do it again? yes but!

- Have a better understanding of the finances, and have all correct paperwork updated pre-assignment.

- Establish and prioritise pre-assignment agreed boundaries on family responsibilities, home leaves.

- Pre-assignment or early into the assignment, in-build into the family calendar and finances, familiarisation and re-connection trips to partner's posting.

What have I learnt?

- Realisation that your relationship is often played out under a microscope, and has to be strong to survive.

- You have to regularly review and re-evaluate your personal and family priorities.

- Why are you doing it? Is it worth it?

- Don't be a martyr! Being the 'stay-at-home' partner is both tiring and can be lonely. Recognise that in your partner's absence, you need a distraction, to compensate for loss of companionship. Join a gym, do an evening class, re-invent your career.

- Not to feel guilty if things do not work out to plan.

- Being a strong character, independent and capable has been very useful, but impossible to keep up 24/7. You must allow yourself some 'off duty time'.

- Periods of self-reflection are essential, you have to be flexible and appreciate that yours is not the only way!

- Always being the disciplinarian with children in your partner's absence, can become a negative and onerous factor.

- The kids have had to develop independence.

- Creation and maintenance of a good support network is essential, if you are prepared to work at it, makes the whole experience easier, and more enjoyable!

- Arrange visits in posting helps breaks the monotony.

- Be aware that your relationship will only continue to prosper and flourish if you are prepared to regularly re-negotiate it! It is very easy for both partners to become too independent and with long absences let the relationship 'drift'.

- If you have a problem don't suffer in silence, talk to a professional.

- Has it enhanced my personal development as well as professional.

- That everyone's contribution to the success of this lifestyle is essential.

Several months ago during a recent 'heated discussion' with Laura aged sixteen the subject of the 'discussion' being homework! Unknowingly she provided a superb analogy and concluding paragraph for the end of the book. In the wonderfully intolerant and forthright manner of adolescents she voiced her opinion thus 'you are like a trapeze artist in a circus, tense, focused and always in control '!.'

This analogy was for me, a perfect illustration of the 'stay at homes' role, on duty, responsible, in control. Like the trapeze artist, responsible, but without the support of a 'safety net' (support network) and participation of the audience, it could prove a lonely and challenging experience.

If you are prepared and accepting that you are pivotal to your family's role and continuing successful balance for the duration of your family's participation in the short term assignment lifestyle, you are well on the way. Remember the process will be a journey for the whole family, each individual's journey will be unique. As with all journeys, there will be periods of calm and storm. As long as you have the appropriate tools to help weather the storms, there will be less resistance, more personal growth, enjoyment, freedom, fun and happiness. None of you will be the same as when you started this process, be accepting of the changes, and celebrate them.

Although as a family we consider ourselves 'veterans of the short term assignment lifestyle', it is only in the last 2 years we have really begun to understand, both as individuals and a family, that although this is a very challenging lifestyle for the whole family, there are also many benefits.

About the Author

"Alone at Home" is Marian Weston's first book, however she already has extensive experience writing for expatriate magazines, newspapers and specialist websites.

Now based in Devon, England, Marian has been able to draw upon more than 25 years of expatriate experience. She was initiated into this unique world when her parents "upped sticks" to work in East Africa and, subsequently, Dubai. It was not long before she and her husband were drawn back to this life, bringing up two young children in the Middle East. Latterly, with her husband Andrew employed on short term assignments overseas, she has experienced a challenging few years as a "stay-at-home partner" back in the UK with the children. . With her eldest successfully settled at university and her youngest grappling with 'A' levels, she now feels it is time to share some of her hard-earned experience of this unusual, difficult and often lonely lifestyle.

Recommendations

"The struggles families face during job assignment separation are real and plentiful. These challenges have gone virtually unrecognized, until now. Marian's book sheds light on many of the emotional and physical challenges families must endure while a loved one is away on assignment. Using her personal experiences to guide her, Marian shares with us important coping strategies and helpful hints for negotiating, nourishing and maintaining family relationships from afar."

Kelley Graham
Mother of 3 and 'stay-at-home' partner
Hudson, Ohio USA

'Utilising two- plus decades of personal expatriate experience as a springboard. Marian Weston takes us beyond what surveys and statistics can tell us about the evolving nature of international careers and living'.

Jennifer Hamm
International freelance journalist

I too was at home alone with two children while my absent husband was away working. I was lucky. My husband was home at the weekends. But how I empathise with Marian Weston and how I agree with all she writes. Whether you are like to share our shoes or manage those who do, this book will be invaluable.

Jo Parfitt
Author of Career in Your Suitcase and Expat Entrepreneur
www.summertimepublishing.com